The Architecture of
THE INDIAN SULTANATES

The Architecture of
THE INDIAN SULTANATES

edited by **Abha Narain Lambah and Alka Patel**

Marg publications

General Editor
PRATAPADITYA PAL

Research Editor
ANNAPURNA GARIMELLA

Executive Editors
SAVITA CHANDIRAMANI
GAYATRI W. UGRA

Text Editor
RIVKA ISRAEL

Editorial Executive
ARNAVAZ K. BHANSALI

Senior Production Executive
GAUTAM V. JADHAV

Production Executive
VIDYADHAR R. SAWANT

Design
KIRTI TRIVEDI

Captions to preliminary pages

Page 1: View of the interior of Iltutmish's tomb in the Qutb Complex, Delhi, an early attempt at building a dome.
Photograph: Abha Narain Lambah.

Page 2: Carved and spiralling water channels in Mandu give a hint of pre-Mughal landscaping.
Photograph: Dinodia Photo Library/Rajesh H. Sharma.

Page 4: Intricate florate and geometrical patterns characterize early sultanate buildings – detail from the Qutb Complex, Delhi.
Photograph: Tanmaya Tathagat.

Page 5: The octagonal tomb wih its corner *chhatri*s, a hallmark of Lodi and Suri architecture.
Photograph: Catherine B. Asher.

Pages 6 and 7: View of the screen along the western *qibla* wall of the Quwwat ul Islam Mosque, Qutb Complex, Delhi.
Photograph: Tanmaya Tathagat.

Vol. 58 No. 1
September 2006

Price: Rs 2500.00 / US$ 66.00

ISBN: 81-85026-75-0

Library of Congress Catalog Card Number:
2006-345043

Marg's quarterly publications receive support from
the Sir Dorabji Tata Trust – Endowment Fund.

Published by J.J. Bhabha
for Marg Publications on behalf of the
National Centre for the Performing Arts at
24, Homi Mody Street, Mumbai 400 001.

Colour and black and white processing by
Reproscan, Mumbai 400 013.

Printed at Silverpoint Press Private Limited,
Mumbai 400 013, India.

CONTENTS

The publication of this volume has been made possible by generous support received from Simon Ray, Indian & Islamic Works of Art, London; and a grant from a friend of Marg who wishes to remain anonymous.

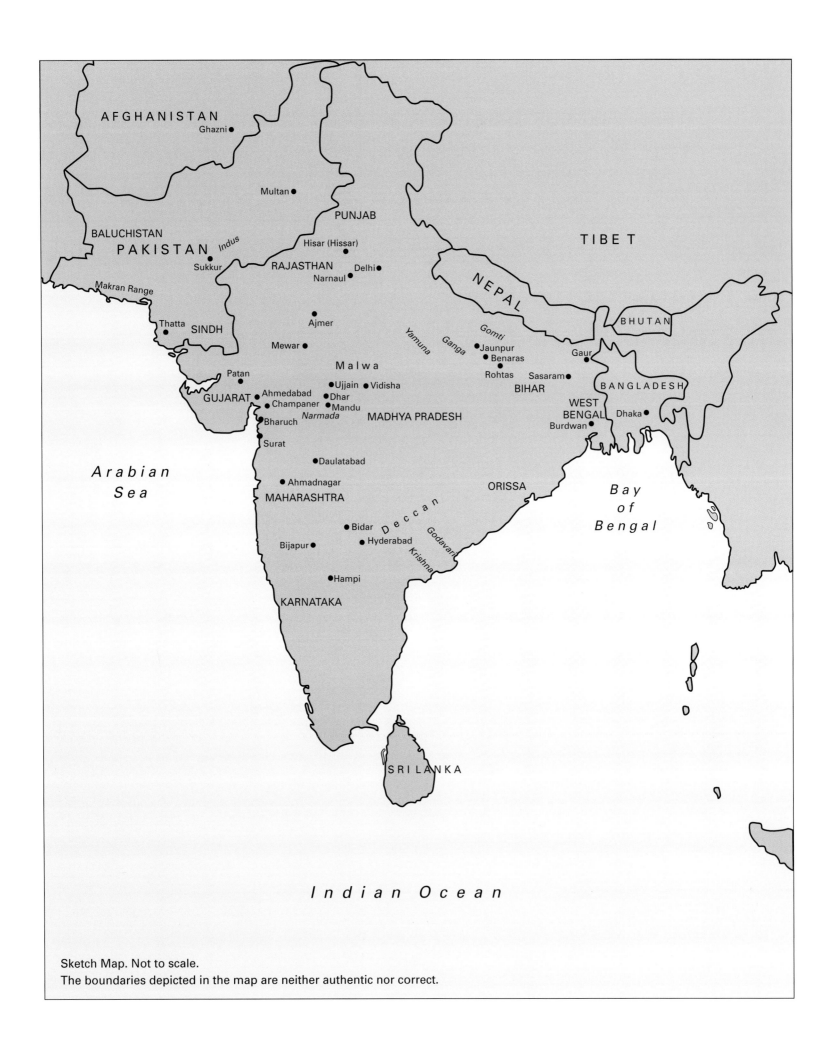

AFGHANISTAN

Ghazni •

Multan •

PUNJAB

BALUCHISTAN

PAKISTAN   Indus

TIBET

Hisar (Hissar) •

RAJASTHAN   Delhi •

NEPAL

Sukkur •

Narnaul •

Makran Range

BHUTAN

Thatta • SINDH

Ajmer •

Mewar •

Malwa

Gomti

Yamuna   Ganga

Jaunpur •

Benaras •

Gaur •

Patan •

Rohtas •

Sasaram •

BANGLADESH

GUJARAT •

Ahmedabad •

Ujjain • Vidisha •

BIHAR

Champaner •

Dhar •

Mandu •

WEST

Bharuch •

Narmada

MADHYA PRADESH

BENGAL   Dhaka •

Surat •

Burdwan •

Arabian
Sea

Daulatabad •

Ahmadnagar •

ORISSA

Bay
of
Bengal

MAHARASHTRA

Bidar •

Deccan

Bijapur •

Hyderabad •

Godavari

Krishna

Hampi •

KARNATAKA

SRI LANKA

Indian Ocean

Sketch Map. Not to scale.
The boundaries depicted in the map are neither authentic nor correct.

Alka Patel

Revisiting the Term "Sultanate"

Thanks to a growing interest in the "Sultanate" or pre-Mughal period of history of the Indian subcontinent, the late 12th through early 16th centuries usually contained in the rubric are undergoing a long awaited process of clarification. Additionally, the rubric itself is at last experiencing definition. For it is curious that, though the term "Sultanate" has been long and commonly used in scholarship with an air of confidence, its chronological and conceptual parameters are far from established. To date, the term loosely corrals a predominantly pre-Mughal Islamic presence in the subcontinent into a deceptively tidy – and ultimately artificial – historical package. But in contrast to all such convenient intellectual constructs, there was much more variation in the political, religious, and architectural landscapes comprising this timeframe than a unitary label such as "the Sultanate period" would indicate.

While the present volume attempts to make usage of the term "Sultanate" more precise, this cannot be achieved without questioning. Thus, at the same time that our work aims to clarify the concepts embodied in the term and their applications, we collectively challenge preconceptions regarding the late 12th through early 16th centuries which have somehow entered lay and scholarly views even though they are not corroborated by the surviving textual and, more especially, architectural evidence. Ultimately, we hope that this work will provide more efficacious tools for the analysis of the early 2nd millennium CE of the region's history, and indeed elucidate whether the legacies of this period extended into the subsequent centuries which are relegated to the Mughals.

The "Sultanate" period is typically defined as beginning with the successful Ghurid incursions into the northern Indian plains in the early 1190s, and ending with the establishment of the house of Babur in 1526. As such, the concept of the "Sultanate" period all too easily and inaccurately encompasses a time of political fragmentation in South Asia, when small, locally based principalities or sultanates were, in a teleological understanding of historical processes, necessary precursors to the Mughal imperium.

The late 12th-century Ghurid annexations of northern India undoubtedly set a historical momentum in motion. Over the next 350 years or so, various dynastic interests from the northwest

1

Ucch Sharif, Pakistan.
Photograph: Alka Patel.

ALKA PATEL

Entrance to the Qala-i-Kuhna
Mosque, Delhi, built by
Sher Shah Sur.
Photograph: Tanmaya Tathagat.

frontiers – motivated at least by pan-Gangetic if not pan-Indic ambitions – made their way into the plains and took up rulership at Delhi. This was the case with the Khaljis in the last quarter of the 13th century, the Tughluqs in the first quarter of the 14th, and ultimately Babur and the Mughals from Ferghana in the third decade of the 16th century. Although these dynasties followed close upon one another's heels, each family's goal was the wresting of power and resources from their predecessors for use exclusively by themselves, their dependants, and their posterity. Indeed, Abha Lambah's paper in this volume vividly sets out an example of these dynastic conflicts in her description of Sikandar Lodi's large-scale destruction of Jaunpur's Sharqi-patronized architecture in 1480, including the eastern and most prominent pylon of the city's congregational mosque (1470). As a result of the varying priorities and consequent antagonisms among the Delhi-based and other regional dynasties, it can be suggested that the plural designation of this period as that of the sultanates, in the lower case, would be more accurate than the capitalized singular "Sultanate" currently used in scholarship.

Pluralization of the rubric to "the period of the sultanates" is further supported as we expand our historical gaze beyond Delhi. Indeed, such an expansion is eminently necessary. We see in Jain-Neubauer's article that Delhi's rise to political prominence came about only during the last decade of the 12th century. Previously, Delhi had been a provincial holding of the Chahamanas of Ajmer. After the defeat of the Chahamana ruler Prithviraja in 1192 at the hands of the Ghurid commander Qutb al-Din Aibek, the ruler's son was left in Ajmer as a feudatory

of the Ghurid sultans. However, Aibek kept a close watch on his new territorial acquisition from nearby Delhi, where he posted a garrison. Although Aibek took direct control of Ajmer in 1198, his presence at Delhi had initiated yet another historical momentum: since the first long-term Islamic power of northern India was based at Delhi, successive Islamic dynasties followed suit, probably for the geopolitical advantage the city offered for control of the areas immediately east of the Indus.

The events described above at Delhi were accompanied by equally prominent contests of power throughout the rest of the subcontinent, in political geography more accurately understood during this period as the sum of its strong regional parts. Centres such as Multan and Ucch Sharif (figure 1) in West Punjab (Pakistan), Anahilvada-Patan (figure 3) and eventually Ahmadabad in Gujarat, Bidar and ultimately Hyderabad in the Deccan, and Gaur in West Bengal all served as sites of political contestation and cultural patronage. These regional capitals, along with their hinterlands, served as stages where dynastic-military interests played out the consolidation of their local power bases and vied for military and political supremacy in the area at least until Mughal annexation, if not beyond. Furthermore, these centres were often only a few among many such locales of patronage furthering the strong, locally based cultural traditions (religious, architectural, textual) of the overall region.

In light of these multiple and simultaneous political events and cultural processes, the singularity of the term "Sultanate" and its wide sweep begin to appear generalizing and oblivious to the political, textual, architectural, and other cultural histories emerging from these regionally based powers. Furthermore, in collapsing the cultural variations in the subcontinent during this period, the capitalized term "Sultanate" in the singular reinforces a teleological conception of history, as noted above. The culmination of this fragmented history was to be political and, by implication, cultural unity throughout the subcontinent. Such a view of the late 12th through 16th centuries, then, also indirectly privileges the Mughal period for its supposed political (if not also cultural) cohesion.

Historical processes, however, are neither predictable nor convenient. The Mughal empire itself was constantly shifting its own boundaries, rarely in a monolithic stasis. This volume's inclusion of

Tomb complex of Sheikh Farid,
Anahilvada-Patan, Gujarat,
15th century.
Photograph: Alka Patel.

Catherine Asher's essay on the mid-16th-century architectural patronage of Sher Shah Sur, who forced the emperor Humayun into exile in Iran for over a decade spanning 1544–55, challenges the image of an unfissured Mughal juggernaut (figure 2). Moreover, while the return of Humayun to the throne of Hindustan in 1555 marked the Mughals' initial push toward territorial expansion and consolidation, with the central region of Malwa already within Mughal control as early as 1562, annexations of outlying regions such as Gujarat did not take place until ten years later in 1572–73, Bengal in 1576, Sindh only in 1591, and the Golconda sultanate over 130 years later in 1687.

The dissemination of Mughal rule was, then, by no means instantaneous. More to the point, it can be acceptably argued that political and cultural cohesion (if it exists) is not a criterion determining analytical worth. Indeed, the great varieties of architectural and other cultural traditions patronized throughout the sultanates, beginning in the late 12th century, all deserve as much individual attention and analysis as the territorially larger Mughal empire.

Past studies of the late 12th through 16th centuries have concentrated, often exclusively, on the Islamic political and material histories of South Asia, thereby implying that little non-Islamic textual or architectural evidence of note survives from the period. By means of in-depth and inclusive analyses of architectural evidence from regional perspectives, the contributors to this volume show this to be far from the case. Holly Edwards' treatment of late 12th-through 14th-century architecture of the Indus Valley demonstrates not only that significant non-Islamic architecture survives there in the form of temples and temple complexes, but also that the formal and iconographic traditions evinced in these were creatively expanded to meet the Islamic demands of predominantly funereal-commemorative buildings. Pika Ghosh's study of the mosques and temples of Bengal, spanning the 14th through 16th centuries, shows that this region's various religious architectures shared many components with the local domestic-vernacular buildings as well.

Both these studies also question the often invoked associations between dynastic patronage and architectural form, as well as that between religion, specifically Islam, and architectural form. Previous works have focused on dynasty and/or religion as formative forces in architectural form and practice,

possibly a continuation of the 19th-century colonial epistemology that infused the study of the Indian subcontinent in general. However, the contributions to this volume – including but not exclusively those on the Indus Valley, West Bengal, and to an extent also Jaunpur – amply illustrate that an inclusive, cross-sectarian, and *regionally* based approach to these building traditions is the historically more accurate and fruitful one.

Perhaps the building that serves as a culmination of the integrity of regionally based architectural traditions during the period of the sultanates is Hyderabad's Charminar (1591). In his analysis of the precedents for this unusual building, Phillip Wagoner demonstrates yet another type of regional integrity in addition to the formal, religious, and sacred-secular continuities we saw earlier: Although the Charminar shares little in the way of either form or function with its typological and functional precedent the *chaubara*, a uniquely Deccani building type, the *chaubara*'s *conceptual* assimilation and innovative application in the Charminar is unmistakable. Wagoner's article serves as a significant methodological example for future works, stressing the fundamental importance of approaching the architectural remains of the sultanates from their own unique, regionally based perspectives.

In summary, then, just as "India" has too often been ahistorically conceived as a land unified by religion, culture, and social customs – essentially justifying its existence as a "nation" – the "Sultanate" period has also been reductively utilized and deployed in scholarship as an undifferentiated entity. The Islamic affiliations and non-indigenous origins of the various dynasties have been the basis for this lack of differentiation. Scholarly discourse has often avoided the dynastic conflicts leading to divisions of territories and new rulerships, inaccurately privileging religion and ethnic origin as the primary axes of affiliation and action. Indeed, it is noteworthy that the so-called Sultanate period has enjoyed such longevity as an intellectual construct – and that in a time such as now, when scholarly methodologies constantly question monolithic definitions. The staying power of this monolith has larger ramifications: it implies that historical complexity is still a luxury reserved principally for discourses on the occidental world. The authors in this volume appropriate this "luxury" for South Asia, with the aim that the work will collectively contribute to differentiating and enriching our apprehensions of the region.

Abha Narain Lambah

The Architecture of the Sultanates: A Historical Prologue

The vast territories of Hindustan offered the builders of the 12th–16th centuries abundant resources of rich building material, as well as skilled craftsmen from hereditary caste guilds. The ritual and non-iconographic needs of Islam demanded a new form and ornamentation. Attempts to craft local trabeate construction to visibly arcuate forms are seen in the screens of the Qutbi complex (figure 1), Ajmer's congregational mosque (known as the Arhai din ka Jhonpra), and other 13th-century monuments. While many sultanates eventually developed the structural vocabulary of arches and vaults, Gujarat's architecture largely continued with post and lintel construction, as argued in Patel's contribution to the present volume.

Two invasions had a great role to play in fashioning the destiny of the Indian sultanates. Ala al-Din Khalji's (r. 1296–1316) fierce resistance to the Mongol invasions established Delhi as a great Islamic court. Later, the invasion by Timur and his sack of Delhi in 1398, dealt the final blow to imperial Tughluq rule. This event led many provinces to declare their independence as sultanates in their own right. Bengal had

1

The arched screen of the Quwwat ul Islam Mosque demonstrating the early Sultanate builders' attempts to craft local trabeate construction to visibly arcuate forms, Qutb complex, Delhi. Photograph: Tanmaya Tathagat.

already declared its independence during the time of Muhammad Tughluq (r. 1325–51), and much of the Deccan was lost by Firuz Shah (r. 1351–88) with the formation of the Vijayanagara empire. With the Tughluq empire reeling under Timur's attack, Malwa, Jaunpur, and Gujarat proclaimed themselves independent sultanates. The following decades witnessed Delhi's distinct architectural exploration as the contributions of the Sayyids (1414–51) and Lodis (1451–1526) were largely limited to sepulchral monuments. With the Mughal invasion in 1526, localized architectural traditions entered into dialogue with a larger imperial language. The short reign of Sher Shah Sur, however, was a brief but important exception, as discussed in Catherine Asher's essay.

For the many rulers of Hindustan during these centuries, their sultanates were perceived as outlying areas of Dar al-Islam, with its centre at least nominally at Abbasid Baghdad and at Cairo by 1261. Recognition and acceptance from this centre was a constant aspiration with sultans sending emissaries to the Abbasid Caliph's court to gain investitures and other honours. It was not until Ala al-Din Khalji that the idea of a pan-Indian rulership emerged, evidenced in his military campaigns in central India and success against Mongol invasions (figure 2). Finally in 1343 during the reign of Muhammad Tughluq, the Abbasid Caliph, now based at Cairo, sent an emissary to recognize him as Sultan, making him the first sultan after Iltutmish to receive formal investiture from the Caliph.

The Tughluqs were the most prolific builders of the Delhi sultanates. Ghiyath al-Din Tughluq (r. 1320–25), Muhammad, and his nephew Firuz Shah were all born to Hindu women, establishing the first recorded Islamic dynasty of at least partly indigenous stock. As discussed in Jain-Neubauer's article, Tughluq

2

It was not until the Alai Darwaza built by Ala al-Din Khalji in 1305 that the dome was successfully constructed. The structure is built as a gateway, not a sepulchral monument, and yet it remains a key link in the development of tomb typology, successfully combining engineering prowess with a sophisticated architectural aesthetic. Photograph: Abha Narain Lambah.

3

Tomb of Ghiyath-al Din
Tughluq, Tughluqabad, Delhi.
Photograph: Jutta Jain.

architecture spelt a true Indianization with the greatest amount of experimentation, innovation, and construction during the 78 years of the dynasty. The architecture of Multan had a decided influence on Tughluq building forms from the tenure of Ghiyath al-Din as governor of Multan. His mausoleum in Delhi (figure 3) is an exemplar in Tughluq proportion and massing, bearing a distinct resemblance to his earlier construction of Rukn-i-Alam's tomb in Multan. His buildings showcase an architecture of battered walls and defensive buttresses of serviceable rubble masonry, illustrating a militaristic, robust masculinity that almost altogether dispensed with trivial ornamentation and was to become the hallmark of Tughluq architecture.

Firuz Shah adopted a policy of appeasement of the Ulemas (Islamic jurists), including the occasional desecration of temples[1] to publicly demonstrate his religious zeal. He left most of the governance to Khan-i Jahan Tilangani and his son Khan-i Jahan Junah Shah, leaving him time for his passion for building. Firuz Shah emerged as the most prolific builder among Delhi's Islamic rulers with a legacy of 50 canals, 40 mosques, 30 colleges, 100 palaces, 1,200

gardens, and 30 towns.[2] He was also a conservationist, restoring the Qutbi Mosque, Sultan Garhi, Qutb Minar, and Ala al-Din Khalji's tank, and 22 mosques, madrasas, and tombs[3] (figure 4).

With the many significant dynastic changes occurring at Delhi during the late 12th through 16th centuries, we might wonder to what degree this *political* centre affected the *architectural* vocabulary of other regions. Even before the demise of the Tughluqs, Gujarat, Jaunpur, Malwa, the Deccan, and Bengal had thriving localized architectural traditions, which went on to yield innovative solutions to building for the region's Islamic communities. However, Jaunpur, in relative proximity to Delhi, maintained an umbilical connection with Tughluq architecture for the 100-odd years of its existence, and Malwa too borrowed architectural concepts from imperial Delhi. Although geographically distant, Daulatabad in the western Deccan evinced a close relationship to the architecture of imperial Delhi. This relationship can be attributed to its brief role as Tughluq capital. Nevertheless, the later Deccan sultanates demonstrate strong regional identities.

4

Firuz Shah Tughluq is credited with having repaired many of the buildings within the Qutb complex. View of Alai Darwaza with Qutb Minar behind. Photograph: Tanmaya Tathagat.

Bengal and Gujarat continued to retain and develop their own architectural and aesthetic identities, challenging the concept of Delhi as fountainhead. For most of the history of the Ahmad-Shahi sultanate (circa 1411–1572), Gujarat remained largely isolated from imperial Delhi. It was brought under Mughal rule by Akbar in 1572. As discussed in Alka Patel's essay, Gujarat's architecture retained a strongly independent trajectory, based on a rich local tradition. Bengal too, with its annexation by Bakhtiyar Khalji in 1204, came under Delhi's rule for a brief period, but its distance from Delhi made its rule by local governors a political necessity. This allowed for its regional style of brick and stucco to flourish, with the mosques at Pandua and Gaur boldly striking out to create their distinctive architectural vocabulary.

Rather than a unidirectional relationship of "influence" from Delhi, the sultanates of the Indian subcontinent witnessed a steady interchange of architectural concepts among themselves. Jaunpur's vaulted buildings show affinity with Bengal. Michael Brand explores the links between Islamic buildings in Mandu and contemporary Hindu and Jain structures in Kumbhalgarh and Ranakpur. This

5

Polychromatic stone work detail
from Ibrahim Sur's tomb at
Narnaul built in the reign of
Sher Shah Sur.
Photograph: Tanmaya Tathagat.

as local building traditions rose to meet the needs of the comparatively new ideology of Islam. The resulting buildings of the many sultanates exhibit varying degrees of negotiation between imported Islamic forms and ornament and the local architectural vocabularies. This process of innovation was witnessed throughout the sultanates, so that the supremacy of Delhi as the sole architectural source is effectively discredited. Although the political events in this important city reverberated far and wide, its architectural events were less compelling. The buildings of the various sultanates discussed throughout this volume attest to the pliability of the local traditions, and their potential for accommodating new social, religious, and political vicissitudes.

NOTES

1.   See Abha Narain Lambah's paper on Jaunpur for the recorded destruction of the Atala Devi temple. Also read A. Fuhrer and W. Smith, *The Sharqi Architecture of Jaunpur with notes on Zafarabad, Sahet-Mahet and other places in the North Western Provinces and Oudh*, Archaeological Survey of India, New Delhi, 1994.

2.   Surendra Sahai, *Indian Architecture: Islamic Period 1192–1857*, Prakash Books, New Delhi, 2004, p. 28.

3.   Firuz wrote in his memoirs, "by the guidance of God, I was led to repair and rebuild the edifices and structures of former kings and ancient nobles, which had fallen into decay, from lapse of time, giving the restoration of these buildings the priority over my (own) building works " (source Anthony Welch quoting *Futuhat-i Firuz Shah*, ed. and trans. S.A. Rashid and M.A. Makhdoomi, Aligarh, n.d.).

4.   See Elizabeth Schotten Merklinger, *Sultanate Architecture of Pre-Mughal India*, Munshiram Manoharlal Publishers, New Delhi, 2005.

mobility of ideas can be explained by the involvement of the humble local craftsman. Craft guilds were well established for centuries, moving from one province to another based on the availability of patrons and commissions. These clans of travelling artisans were responsible for the fluidity of architectural forms throughout the sultanates including Delhi and the other courts. Indeed, the 1398 sack of Delhi by Timur's armies also resulted in the dispersal of craftsmen to other patrons as they sought refuge and work.

Merklinger[4] refers to five dynasties and 34 sultans of the "Sultanate"; she is one of many authors who put forward a pre-Mughal definition of the term. This volume stretches the definition over a time line to include the Suri dynasty. The architecture of the Suris, though chronologically post-establishment of the Mughal dynasty, is yet integrally a part of the development of the architecture of the sultanates, with the minor interruption of Babur's and Humayun's constructions. Sher Shah Sur's prolific building works, which extend all the way from Sindh through to Bihar, exhibit indigenous regional characteristics (figure 5). As is underscored by the essays in this volume, the articulation of regional traditions is one of the hallmarks of the architecture of the sultanates.

Thus, the period of the sultanates constitutes a time of unprecedented architectural experimentation

Holly Edwards

Centralizing the Margins: Commemorative Architecture in the Indus Valley

The tomb of Rukn al-Din Rukn-i-Alam in Multan, Pakistan (figure 2) has elicited rhapsodic descriptions as well as more sober comment, but whatever the individual writer's stance, everyone acknowledges the monument's art historical significance. The building was the focus of an award-winning restoration campaign some years ago[1] and it has generated sustained comment in scholarly literature as well. A rigorous monographic study of the Multan tomb published in 1992, for example, described the structure as "the finest Islamic mausoleum of pre-Mughal India", a "triumphant and profoundly original synthesis of two related styles, those of the Iranian world and the subcontinent", holding a "commanding position in Sultanate architecture".[2] A textbook enshrined the monument as "the earliest example of Tughluq architecture", noting its commission by Ghazi Malik Tughluq (later Ghiyath al-Din Tughluq) when he was provincial governor of the area.[3] I too would like to underscore the significance of the structure but in a somewhat unconventional manner, for while the tomb manifests a refinement comparable to monuments of imperial patronage, the vernacular context of the shrine and its relation to other sultanate traditions deserves further scrutiny.

That the building's humble roots have escaped sustained attention is consistent with the priorities of traditional art historical discourse. For present purposes, that tradition might be summarized as follows: the arcuate brickworking traditions of Iran/Central Asia intersected with the trabeate ashlar styles of India in the wake of the Ghurid conquest of the northern subcontinent, giving rise to styles that were fostered and refined in centres of dynastic power and dimly perceived or brilliantly furthered in the provinces. The lynchpin and pivot of this mode of analysis is, of course, Ghurid Delhi around 1200, wherein the "Quwwat ul Islam" often serves to emblematize an implicit conceptual fusion of architectural form, religious conflict, and political hegemony. Within this analytical matrix, the typical path follows the vector of Islam to political power, and thence to architectural history. In the process, visually disparate structures such as the tomb of Rukn-i-Alam and the monuments of Tughluq Delhi are absorbed into a unified narrative as the "Sultanate" chapter of Indo-Islamic architecture.

1

Tomb of Suhagen. Sukkur, Sindh, Pakistan.

2

Tomb of Rukn-i-Alam. Multan, Punjab, Pakistan.

This approach is generating critical scrutiny and revision. What was once thought of as a datable confrontation between hostile faiths has now been stretched into a more protracted, less combative, and arguably dialogic encounter.[4] Ghurid Delhi remains central to this revised scenario[5] but the tomb of Rukn-i-Alam and the cultural continuum with which it is associated deserves attention. Often marginalized or relegated to "provincial" status in relation to Delhi or political centres to the northwest, the Multan region offers the opportunity to study a "frontier" in which a conjunction of religion and political power was not deterministic and architecture was a function of local needs and tastes. Such a project drives a useful wedge between dynastic patronage and architectural history and demonstrates that vernacular building practices, though modest, may ultimately generate masterpieces.

To begin, the integrity and unique character of architectural sequences in the Indus Valley must be appreciated. More than a decade after the studies cited above, the Multan tomb is more widely recognized as the centrepiece of a considerably longer and more variegated regional tradition. Ahmad Nabi Khan, synthesizing this material in his most exhaustive study to date, itemizes a large group of these distinctive commemorative buildings, epitomized by the tomb of Rukn-i-Alam and celebrated as "the Pakistani style", dating from the 14th to the 20th century.[6] While documentation of these structures adds considerably to the corpus of "Indo-Islamic" architecture in general, the genesis and character of this regional style and its relationship to other architectural modes arguably destabilizes traditional canons and chronologies.

Secondly, while scholars in various disciplines are gradually dismantling monolithic entities like "Islam" in favour of more nuanced descriptors, what this means for the study of "Islamic" architecture in the Indus Valley is significant, for it seems to call into question the very narrative within which architecture is contextualized. Art historians typically sketch a sequence of Muslim invasions documented in texts (i.e. Arab, Ghaznavid, Ghurid) in order to structure time and map political terrain[7] in the region prior to the period of the sultanates. Extant architecture is then correlated with political chronologies and presumed sources of patronage and "influence". With reference to other kinds of evidence, including folklore, numismatics, archaeology, and material evidence, however, one can begin to assemble a rather different picture, one in which political power in the region was diffuse and decentralized, and local devotional activities blurred and shifted over time, absorbing Sunnism, Ismailism, Hinduism, worship of the sun and the river Indus, laid over vestiges of Buddhism and Zoroastrianism. This complex scenario in turn gave rise to a discrete architectural tradition, but first some remarks about the cultural milieu.

Perhaps the most distinctive aspect of the Indus Valley's unique ethos is the veneration for the river Indus among Muslims and Hindus alike. In its original form, the cult involved a set of cyclical rituals involving water and light, but at a certain point the river deity came to be personified and architecturally enshrined[8] at two main sites, one at Udero Lal in southern Sindh[9] and another once situated on an island in the middle of the river at Sukkur in northern Sindh.[10] This figure is called by a variety of names (e.g. Udero Lal, Shaikh Tahir, Zenda Pir, and Khwaja Khizr) and inspires diverse forms of homage, some resonant with Muslim funeral rites and others recalling Hindu puja, all enacted around the central "grave" at the shrine of Udero Lal. The shrine upriver marked the site of the last appearance of the saint, and as such, it lacked a grave.

If the entire spectrum of popular piety is synchronically reflected at the shrines of Udero Lal, it may also be diachronically evident in the history of a particular community. Qureshi has argued that the Sumros of Sindh, for example, underwent a chameleon-like transformation from Hinduism through heterodox and orthodox Ismailism to reach an eventual Sunnism.[11] Similarly, Richard Eaton has examined the "Islamization" of the Siyal Jats under the auspices of the Saint Baba Farid Ganj Shakar, whose extraordinarily popular shrine stands in modern Pakpattan, arguing that what was traditionally described as mass conversion at the hands of the saint himself in the 13th century was in fact a process that transpired over 400 years.[12] For the individual or family, moreover, it was likely an unconscious and gradual transition.

3

Tomb of Muhammad ibn Harun. Bela, Baluchistan, Pakistan.

Similarly, prominent political centres of the pre-Sultanate period, often presumed to be "Muslim", also seem to have been sites of confessional pragmatism, each one finding functional stasis for its own particular constituencies. Muslims held nominal (minority) control of the long-established city of Multan, for example, by co-opting the tremendously popular and lucrative shrine to the sun;[13] a much younger city like Mansura was, by contrast, simply a haven for Muslim refugees. The population of Nandana in the Salt Range, the site of al-Biruni's observations of the sun, seems to have run the gamut of faiths, with the remnants of a mosque, a temple, and a stupa in the close confines of a hilltop setting.[14]

Even numismatic evidence of the Ghaznavid move into the subcontinent – spearheaded by that "hammer of heretics" and idol-smasher Mahmud of Ghazni and often cited as a formative Muslim influence – suggests that faith was not necessarily the cause of social cleavage. Coinage clearly intended for the Indian domains often employed Sanskrit along with Arabic legends and often incorporated Shiva's bull as well as the phrase *Sri Samantadevi*. Some mintings continued a well established type in the subcontinent, particularly the Hindu Shahi "Bull and Horseman" series;[15] this was not a numismatic imposition of dogma but rather an effort simply to interpolate economic exchange into a new register.

Such disparate evidence cumulatively suggests that, "on the ground", the Indus Valley incubated a spectrum of piety, in which there were poles and intermediate gradations but few rigid or exclusionary boundaries. In this terrain, political power was atomized and pragmatic and religion was not a cultural fault line. How was this ethos reflected in local building practices?

To answer this question, one might begin by noting a relative dearth of elaborate mosque architecture, a building form inherently politicized and centred in the collectivities of institutionalized Islam.[16] There is, by contrast, a plethora of tomb structures dedicated to local heroes, teachers, or saints – the archetype being of course, the shrine of Rukn-i-Alam – many of which are undocumented and renovated. Despite their often refurbished states, these monuments attest to the deeply rooted commemorative tradition of recording local history through architecture. The shrine of Udero Lal discussed above, the tomb of Chuto Amrani and that of Haji ibn Turabi,[17] are representative samples of this

phenomenon; though their original appearance is often obscured behind layers of whitewash and structural additions, their fundamental similarity to unrenovated monuments (to be discussed below) lends credence and depth to our reconstitution of the intertwined devotional and architectural traditions.

For purely art historical purposes, however, a group of related commemorative structures dotting the riparian landscape are particularly useful in that they manifest a shared vocabulary of structural and decorative features in untouched form. All are modest domed squares enshrining heroes or other venerated figures of the early eras of Islam in the region. The tomb of Muhammad ibn Harun, thought to be the

4

Detail of brick cornice, tomb of Muhammad ibn Harun. Bela, Baluchistan, Pakistan.

earliest extant Muslim commemorative monument in the Indus Valley[18] is a useful point with which to begin (figure 3). It stands in rolling country at the edge of the deserts of Makran in southern Pakistan. The main personage enshrined in the tomb is an individual of considerable celebrity among the early heroes of Islam in the Indus Valley. Credited with bringing Makran under caliphal control and forerunner to Muhammad ibn Qasim (who is credited, in turn, with the Arab "conquest" of Sindh), Muhammad ibn Harun died in AH 92. If he is clearly remembered as a major figure in local history, however, neither the patron nor the date of his tomb is well documented.[19]

The tomb consists of a domed square, constructed entirely of brick and mud mortar. While it has been refurbished, pre-restoration photographs suggest that the work was respectful of the building's original appearance.[20] The lower walls are relatively plain, punctuated by recesses and flat pilasters, visually supporting a wide textile-like cornice of carved brickwork (figure 4). This elaborate band derives its

decorative character from carved bricks, conventionally laid. What distinguishes these bricks, one from the other, is the manner in which their narrow exposed edge is treated. In addition to the plain brick, there are five carved variants including the diamond chain, the continuous zigzag, the sawtooth, the half moon, and the plain brick with notches cut in the ends. Using the last two types, more complex shapes were also rendered across lay lines. For example, by inverting the half-moon in a second lay above the first and shifting it slightly sidewards, a continuous waving line was formed; similarly two half-moons might be joined with a lay of notched bricks in between to create what will hereafter be termed a pearl chain.

Inside the structure, another feature deserves comment – the transition zone supporting the dome. This consists of four squinches of distinctive form: voussoir arches bridge the structural gap between the square space of the interior and the dome ring. These arches are supplemented with a pendentive-like zone

5

Anonymous tomb. Aror, Sindh, Pakistan.

of protruding dentils which serve to bring the wall surface forward to the plane of the arch itself. This squinch type effectively conjoins arcuate and trabeate building strategies to support the weight of the dome (see figure 6 for comparable form).

Several observations follow. First, this squinch form, bearing functional but not aesthetic resemblance to equivalent architectural elements in monuments to the north and west, and the cut brickwork manifest a striking and organic intimacy between material, structure, and decoration. With very modest means, the builder created a viable though quite spare interior space and a distinctive exterior articulation. This is arguably the very essence of vernacular architecture

6
Detail of squinch. Aror, Sindh, Pakistan.

7

Patan Manara. Rahimyar Khan,
Sindh, Pakistan.

and localized craft tradition. Moreover, a familial resemblance between this structure and the tomb of Rukn-i-Alam, suggested by decorative and structural commonalities such as the pearl chain and waving lines, brick serving ornamental and structural roles and domed commemorative space, invites a consideration of what intervenes between the modest tomb and the grand shrine. The intermediate steps can be traced with reference to a few more buildings.

The features noted in reference to the tomb of Muhammad ibn Harun occur again, in an anonymous tomb in Aror (figure 5), further north in the watershed. This structure stands in the middle of an open area near the Nara canal, a diversion which runs southeast from the river at Sukkur. The building stands a short distance south of a large mound, which is thought to be the city of Aror, Al-Ror, or Alor,[21] the administrative centre of Sindh on the eve of the first Muslim incursions. It had been the seat of the Buddhist Rai dynasty, in turn usurped by the Hindu Chach and then eventually conquered by Muhammad ibn Qasim in 711 CE. Subsequently straddling the borders between two different centres of political gravity, Mansura and Multan, the town enjoyed a mercantile prosperity due to riverine trade until such time as the riverbed shifted westward, leaving Aror marooned.[22]

This little-known structure is essentially an enlarged and elaborated version of the tomb of Muhammad ibn Harun though the exterior walls exhibit somewhat more elaborate treatment in three zones – a dado zone consisting of recessed arches culminating in crosses and merlons, a pilastered intermediate zone, and a textile-like cornice band. This cornice zone is the only part of the structure executed in fine carved brickwork which contrasts in both texture and colour with the rest of the tomb. In its present state, it consists of about sixteen lays, in which various different patterns alternate with courses of plain brick; they include a pearl chain, a waving line, a diamond chain, another waving line, and fretwork of small crosses. Inside, atop basically plain brick walls, the dome rests on squinches which chamfer the corners with pointed arches; like those of the tomb of Muhammad ibn Harun, these arches are supplemented with a cone of corbelling dentils which serve to inch the wall surface forward to meet the back of the arch proper (figure 6). The corners of the square space, then, are "filled in" as well as arched over.

Uniting these two modest monuments is a distinctive approach to a commonplace material: brick. Both buildings capitalize on the decorative potential as well as the structural versatility of the individual brick. It can be plain and prosaic or carved and assembled into larger pattern; it can also function in diverse ways to oversail empty space, functioning both in trabeate and arcuate modes. Local building practices, then, arise organically from applying readily available materials to structural need and commemorative purpose.

Two other anonymous structures[23] in nearby Sukkur, of which one is shown here (figure 1), are stylistically related though they display considerably enhanced exterior surface complexity. The fine brick revetment, previously confined to the cornice, becomes a continuous skin on the outside of the building articulated into three zones: a dado-like base of multiple mouldings supporting a series of pilasters which in turn support a decorative cornice very like that of the preceding structures but with a larger vocabulary of motifs. The interiors remain quite bare of decoration and the domes are supported by "filled in squinches". While one might dwell at greater length on the expanded decorative repertoire, for present purposes, the general stylistic continuities demonstrate the conservative pace and momentum of indigenous building practices.

This group of relatively anonymous tomb structures must, in turn, be positioned within a larger context of material evidence. Art historians have chosen to seek formative influence along the vector of faith, specifically in the Ghaznavid realm and further north/west, where brick is a common material and Islam is the common faith. Recent scholarship[24] however foregrounds a distinctive decorative repertoire from Ghaznavid monuments, including vegetal motifs, fields of geometric pattern, and extensive epigraphy which is entirely lacking in the Indus Valley sequence. Thus, while there is generic similarity between two regional brickworking traditions, the parallel does not appear to be a formative axis.

As an alternative strategy, it seems appropriate to point to resonances among diverse structures in the immediate region which manifest comparable aesthetic choices and building procedures. Within the Indus Valley watershed, a variety of structures share certain programmatic features noted in relation to the tombs, namely decoration concentrated on the exteriors while the interiors exhibit bare walls;

distinctive techniques of covering interior spaces; and façades articulated in horizontal zones with a dado/plinth level, a middle zone punctuated with pilasters or other vertical dividers, and a cornice/superstructure of denser patterning. Various Hindu monuments in the Salt Range such as Malot, Kafir Kot, Amb, Kallar, Nandana, exhibit these features with varying degrees of consistency.[25] The brickwork of Patan Manara (figure 7), for example, is particularly comparable to the smooth brickwork and mouldings of the Aror tombs, while the temples of Kafir Kot (figure 8) exhibit decorative programmes and structural features similar to the Sukkur monuments. Stupas in the area,

8

Temple at Kafir Kot. Salt Range, Punjab, Pakistan.

9
Ribat of Ali ibn Karmakh.
Kabirwalla, Punjab, Pakistan.

such as Manikala and Guldara,[26] exhibit similar façade compositions though they obviously lack interior spaces.

If vernacular building in the Indus Valley offers the craft traditions and basic features of subsequent monumental architecture, the passage of Ghurid contingents through the region[27] facilitated the transmission of exotic elements into the architectural repertoire from relative proximity and through textually recorded encounter. In seeking to more fully understand the iconic tomb of Rukn-i-Alam, two particular features – its turreted silhouette and its vivid glazed tilework – find meaningful precedents in architecture epigraphically linked to specific Ghurid patrons. The former appears very close at hand in a monument commissioned by Ali ibn Karmakh, a prominent figure in the Ghurid entourage. Standing a relatively short distance from Multan, this structure manifests the aesthetic of fortification of the Ghurid heartland, somewhat incongruously transplanted to the less rugged riverine landscape (figure 9).[28]

The other exotic element of the tomb of Rukn-i-Alam which is critical to its aesthetic character is the tilework which enhances the exterior.[29] The operative precedent for this also lies in Ghurid architecture, manifest for example in the well known tower of Jam.[30] With glazed inscriptions that identify the Ghurid monarch Ghiyath al-Din Muhammad ibn

Sam (r. 1163–1203), the tower demonstrates the existence of tilemaking technology as nearby as the Ghurid heartland.

If it is reasonable to point to this proximate source for technical advance and fortified style, it is less reasonable to suppose that the absorption of these elements into the continuum of vernacular building practices in the Indus Valley was immediate or fundamentally transformative. Evidence of an incremental and even superficial process emerges at a necropolis in the central Punjab known as Lal Mahra Sharif. While this controversial site deserves detailed study,[31] some general comments suffice here.

The site stands on a flood-plain west of the Dera Ismail Khan/Taunsa Sharif road, encompassing four standing structures and other diverse material remains. A few general points about the largest of the monuments (figure 10) serve present purposes well:

First, it exhibits a familiar vocabulary of decorative motifs – waving lines, pearl chains – as well as structural features – modest scale and "filled in" squinches. These features, moreover, are executed with a familiar vernacular modesty, with structure and decoration emerging organically from the layline and potential of common bond brickwork. The tomb, however, is also notably different from its predecessors, enhanced by glazed tilework and buttressing corner

turrets. What is important for present purposes, however, is that these new features are grafted onto well established forms in a relatively uncomplicated way. Colour highlights traditional pearl chains and waving lines and enlivens the monochrome brick surfaces; turrets reinforce the corners of buildings of a still simple plan. That these new features are rendered or absorbed in a somewhat tentative manner is evident in the blurred and imperfect glazings of individual tiles.

If it is a relatively short geographic and art historical jump to the tomb of Rukn-i-Alam from here, what have we learned in the process? First, by acknowledging the formative potential of vernacular traditions, the character of a grand monument can be appreciated as the organic extension of local practice rather than dynastic patronage or distant "influence".

Individual decorative motifs, building materials, domed and turreted silhouette, and commemorative purpose all find precedent in the immediate vicinity. Secondly, such a perspective entails a re-valencing of religion and dynastic patronage as key factors in architectural history; even as distinctions between faiths were blurred in both devotional and building practice, so were lines of "influence" from elsewhere. Finally, by positioning the tomb of Rukn-i-Alam as the zenith of a regional tradition, fertilized by the passage of Ghurid contingents through the area, the unique and iconic status of this remarkable monument can be more accurately appreciated.

PHOTO CREDITS
All photographs by the author.

10

Lal Mahra Sharif. Punjab, Pakistan.

NOTES

1. The building won the Aga Khan Award for Restoration in 1983. The renovation is discussed in Muhammad Wali Ullah Khan, *Mausoleum of Shaikh Rukn-e-Alam*, Multan, Lahore, 1985; Sherban Cantacuzino, ed., *Architecture in Continuity: Building in the Islamic World Today*, New York, 1985, pp. 172–77.

2. Robert Hillenbrand, "Turco-Iranian Elements in the Medieval Architecture of Pakistan: The Case of the Tomb of Rukn-i-Alam at Multan", *Muqarnas,* vol. 9 (1992), pp. 148–74.

3. Sheila Blair and Jonathan Bloom, *The Art and Architecture of Islam, 1250–1800*, New Haven, 1994, p. 151. The association of the tomb with the Tughluq ruler is problematical. See Hillenbrand, footnote 32.

4. See an overview of these efforts in Richard Eaton, ed., *India's Islamic Traditions, 711–1750*, Oxford, 2003, pp. 1–34.

5. See, for example, Finbarr B. Flood, "Refiguring Islamic Iconoclasm: Image Mutilation and Aesthetic Innovation in the Early Mosque", in Anne L. McLanan and Jeffrey Johnson, eds., *Negating the Image: Case Studies of Past Iconoclasms*, London, 2003.

6. Ahmad Nabi Khan, *Islamic Architecture in South Asia: Pakistan – India – Bangladesh*, Oxford University Press, Karachi, 2003, pp. 54–65.

7. Ahmad Nabi Khan uses this format; see note 6. For a more protracted study of historical sources see Holly Edwards, "The Genesis of Islamic Architecture in the Indus Valley", unpublished Ph.D. dissertation, Institute of Fine Arts, New York University, 1990.

8. Sociological documentation by V.T. Thakur, *Sindhi Culture*, University of Bombay Publications, Sociology Series no. 9, Bombay, 1959, pp. 129–34.

9. This unpublished site consists of the pir's tomb and a miraculous tree incorporated into the southwest corner of a large fort-like structure. Standing separately, another building shelters a well and waterwheel. Although the grave site was presumably earlier, the monumental architectural ensemble is clearly Mughal in date. Edwards, pp. 430–36.

10. This marks the site where Zenda Pir/Khwaja Khizr made his last miraculous appearance. The shrine was washed away in a flood some decades ago, but colonial-period descriptions and photographs suggest that the original building was comparable in form to others discussed here. J.W. Smyth, *Gazetteer of the Province of Sind B* Volume II: Sukkur District, Bombay, 1919, pp. 48–50; Henry Cousens, *The Antiquities of Sind*, Calcutta, 1929, pp. 144–49, pls. lxxv–lxxvii and figure 23.

11. Ishtiaq Husain Qureshi, *The Muslim Community of the Indo-Pakistan Subcontinent (610–1947)*, Karachi, 1977, pp. 28–59.

12. Richard M. Eaton, "The Political and Religious Authority of the Shrine of Baba Farid", in Barbara Daly Metcalf, ed., *Moral Conduct and Authority*, Berkeley, 1984.

13. Edwards, pp. 359–64.

14. Edwards, pp. 323–28.

15. E. Thomas, "On the coins of the kings of Ghazni", *Journal of the Royal Asiatic Society*, vol. ix (1848), viii–xii, pp. 307–10; E. Thomas, "Supplemental Contributions to the Series of the Coins of the Kings of Ghazni" *Journal of the Royal Asiatic Society*, vol. 17 (1860), no. 17. For an overview of related issues see P.C. Roy, *The Coinage of Northern India*, New Delhi, 1980, pp. 90–91.

16. Obviously there are some, including those of Banbhore, Mansura, and Rajagirha. See Ahmad Nabi Khan, pp. 2–4, 18.

17. See Edwards: for Chuto Amrani, pp. 437–45; for Haji ibn Turabi, pp. 446–49.

18. Ahmad Nabi Khan, pp. 38–39; Edwards, pp. 366–79.

19. The few scholars who have ventured suggestions converge on the Ghaznavid period as the most likely time frame: Most recently, Ahmad Nabi Khan dates it to the Ghaznavid period, specifically the 11th century. Khan, p. 49.

20. The building was restored by Pakistan's Department of Archaeology and Museums in the late 1970s. The following remarks are based on a comparison of its present appearance with pre-restoration photographs provided to me by Niaz Rasool, to whom I am indebted.

21. Cf. Mumtaz Pathan, *Arab Kingdom of Al Mansurah in Sind*, Sind, 1974, pp. 103–04 and sources cited therein.

22. Rasheed Bhatti, "Rise and fall of Arore – the Old Capital of Sind", *Sindological Studies*, Summer 1978, pp. 53ff.; Edwards, pp. 383–86.

23. There are two very similar structures standing in close proximity. One of them is reproduced here as the tomb of Suhagen. Ahmad Nabi Khan publishes these buildings with different names: the tomb of Khatal al-din and the tomb of Shakarganj. Khan, pp. 42–43; Edwards, pp. 387–400.

24. E.g. Ralph Pinder-Wilson, "Ghaznavid and Ghurid Minarets", *Iran Journal of British Institute of Persian Studies,* vol. 39 (2001), pp. 155–86; Robert Hillenbrand, "The Architecture of the Ghaznavids and the Ghurids", in Carole Hillenbrand, ed., *Studies in Honor of Clifford Edmund Bosworth*, Leiden, 2000, pp. 124–206.

25. The Hindu monuments of the Salt Range and related structures have increasingly attracted scholarly attention, much of which is currently unavailable to me. These remarks are made on the basis of my own fieldwork. Edwards, pp. 269–364.

26. Edwards, pp. 297–317.

27. A rigorous study of the Ghurid passage and presence in the Indus Valley is provided in Finbarr B. Flood, "Ghurid Architecture in the Indus Valley", *Ars Orientalis*, vol. xxxi (2001), pp. 129–66.

28. H. Edwards, "The ribat of 'Ali b. Karmakh", *Iran,* vol. 29 (1991), pp. 85–94.

29. For a more sustained discussion of the introduction of tilework into the region, see Edwards, pp. 245–54.

30. Janine Sourdel-Thomine, *Le Minaret Ghurid de Jam: Un Chef d'oeuvre du XII siecle*, Paris, 2004; Finbarr B. Flood, review, *Art Bulletin*, vol. lxxxvii, No. 3 (2005), pp. 536–43.

31. For a general description of the site and an overview of diverse theories, see Flood (see note 27), p. 163 and note 80.

Jutta Jain-Neubauer

The Many Delhis:
Town Planning and Architecture
under the Tughluqs (1320–1413)

Introduction

None of the early rulers in India can boast of such extensive town-planning and architectural activity as the Tughluqs. Although the Tughluq dynasty ruled for less than a hundred years, it founded four large towns in the Delhi area and three outside, building numerous religious and civic buildings and institutions in the process, such as roads and bridges, caravanserais, and stepwells, as well as hospitals and orchards.

In 1192 the Chahamana ruler Prithviraja II, who had ruled parts of Rajasthan and Delhi from his capital at Ajmer was defeated by the Ghurid commander Qutb al-Din Aibek, and executed at the order of the Ghurid sultan Muizzuddin Muhammad. Thereafter, Islamic rule began in northern India. The son of Prithviraja II continued at Ajmer as a feudatory of the Ghurids, while Aibek stationed himself at Delhi, then one of the provincial holdings of the Chahamanas. It was only with the long-term presence of Aibek's garrison that Delhi was transformed from an important but peripheral city to an imperial capital, thereafter serving as the centre of power for successive Delhi sultanates.

This essay explores the ideas behind Tughluq town-planning and the morphology and urban architecture of the Tughluq township, as far as this is possible from the available historical sources and extant sites. As such, the first section treats the Tughluqs' role in uniting the fragmented urban pockets of Delhi and raising them to metropolitan and imperial status, in the context of the social, economic, and political framework of the time. The second section is concerned with the architecture and planning of the bipartite system of the Tughluq town, tracing the evolution of its distinct division between the space of the fortified seat of power and the space of its inhabitants.

1

Begumpuri Masjid, *qibla iwan*, facing the direction of Mecca. Photograph: Tanmaya Tathagat.

I. The Tughluq Ascendancy

The centuries preceding Tughluq rule were marked by the establishment and expansion of the first Turkic-Islamic principalities in India. Their rulers brought with them sophisticated engineering skills, a well-established tradition of town-planning, and ambitious architectural visions[1] incorporating complex dome constructions, vaults and pointed arches for mosques, mausolea, fortified palaces, and civic buildings. The new rulers also attracted traders, religious scholars, architects, engineers, and specialized craftsmen to Delhi and other seats of power.

Ibn Batuta describes the Tughluqs as originally belonging to a Turkic tribe which came to India and through intermarriage became assimilated in their new homeland.[2] The dynastic cognomen Tughluq[3] derives from the personal name of its first ruler, Ghazi Malik or Ghazi Beg Tughluq. According to the *Tughluqnama*[4] the name was known among the Mongols. The Tughluqs not only continued West Asian and Iranian models in town-planning and architecture, but also evolved a mature and confident style of their own in India.

Their first ruler, Ghiyath al-Din Tughluq (r. 1320–25), rose to the throne at a time when widespread political insecurity characterized much of northern India, partly due to the numerous attacks carried out by the Mongols during the 13th century. According to the writer and poet Amir Khusrau (1253–1325), Ghiyath al-Din had been a military officer in the service of Jalal al-Din Khalji, who appointed him governor of Dipalpur near Multan, southwest Punjab, after he successfully defended his territory against Mongol invasions.

Although the reigns of the first three Tughluq sultans were marked by alternating periods of peace and instability, each of them was a skilful administrator of the state and of society, and ardent patron of the arts and architecture. Ghiyath al-Din Tughluq ascended the throne at Delhi in 1320 as an aged man and was to rule for only five years. Considered to be a prudent ruler and far-sighted political administrator, he began to consolidate the authority of the Tughluq sultanate of Delhi as well as expanding it towards southern and eastern India. He brought relative peace and prosperity to the territory after years of turmoil.

The brief but crucial rule of Ghiyath al-Din was followed by the ascendance of the despotic Muhammad (r. 1325–51). He is remembered for the transfer of his capital from Delhi to Daulatabad (1326–27), and again back to Delhi. On his death he was succeeded by his nephew Firuz Shah (r. 1351–88), the third Tughluq sultan. Firuz Shah was less a statesman and more a prolific patron of the arts and architecture. In his autobiography, *Futuhat-i Firuz Shah*, he writes that one of his greatest personal assets was his desire to build public buildings and civic facilities to make the lives of his subjects more comfortable and prosperous.[5] A great planner, he founded a number of new urban settlements and constructed a network of canals and tanks, wells and stepwells, and gardens and orchards. He also regulated trade and commerce. Hence it would be accurate to call Firuz Shah the master-planner and builder of the

2

"The eight cities of Delhi", by S. Lal, 1945, reproduced from Hilary Waddington, "Adilabad. A part of the 'fourth' Delhi", in *Ancient India*, no. 1, January 1946.

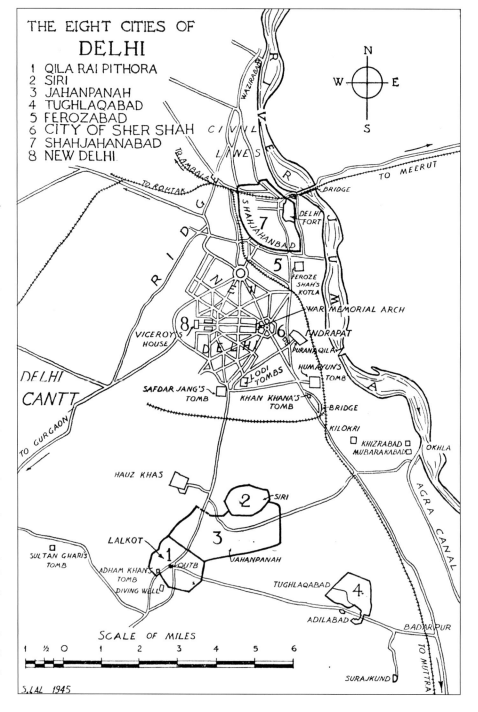

Tughluq dynasty. With his improvements, the state was returned to relative stability and prosperity after Muhammad's despotic reign. Firuz Shah's passion to set up an efficient infrastructure for the benefit of the people makes him one of the greatest visionaries of medieval India.

After the reigns of these sultans came a period of decline and disruption. When Delhi was sacked by Timur in 1398, the Tughluq sultanate effectively came to an end. Yet, during the brief century of predominance, the Tughluq rulers left a profound mark on India's architectural landscape, which would provide a crucial impetus for rulers and aristocracies to come.

The Tughluqs' interaction with the local population was substantial. Social, religious, and physical spaces were continually negotiated in a dynamic dialogue. Economic adjustments often received priority over social or religious considerations. The wealthy and influential Hindu and Jain families, mostly belonging to the trading and money-lending communities, obtained endowments for their temples and acceptance of their professional enterprises, religious activities, and exuberant lifestyles, in exchange for their financial support to the sultans' endeavours. Their protected status within the sultanate is attested by various examples, including of the Jain monastery named Sultan Sarai in honour of the sultan. The Tughluq ruler had returned a confiscated Jain idol to the community. Even Sultan Muhammad was addressed as Maharajadhiraja Shri Mahammada in Jain religious texts.[6]

The Urban Conglomerate Called "Delhi"

Delhi was known to many travellers from other parts of the world during the 13th and 14th centuries. It was described as a prosperous, vibrant, flourishing, well functioning city full of pleasant gardens. It had become "the world's cupola of Islam, leaving behind even Mecca".[7] The north-African traveller Ibn Batuta visited Delhi in 1334, and mentioned that it consisted of four contiguous cities, namely Old Delhi (which during the 12th century was around Rai Pithora), Siri, Tughluqabad, and Jahanpanah. Describing Delhi's grandeur, he says:

"On the next day we arrived at the royal residence of Dihli, the metropolis of the land of al-Hind, a vast and magnificent city, uniting beauty with strength. It is surrounded by a wall whose equal is not known in any country in the world, and is the largest city in India, nay rather the largest of all the cities of Islam in the East."[8]

In the 13th and 14th centuries the city already encompassed a vast area of about 40 square kilometres. Its boundaries encircled the ancient town of Indarpat (Indraprastha) in the north, believed to have been located near present-day Purana Qila on the Yamuna river, to what was then known as Qila Rai Pithora in the south (see figure 2). This whole conglomerate was a heterogeneously settled area consisting of many urban centres. These centres did not remain static over time, but shifted according to the seat of royalty and power. They were well connected by an efficient network of roads and public carriages.[9]

Qila Rai Pithora was where Ala al-Din Khalji ascended the throne of Delhi on October 21, 1296, in the White Palace (Qasri Safed) of Iltutmish. He lived in the Red Palace (Qasri Lal) of Balban, until his own new palace, the "Hazaar Sutun" or Thousand Pillars, was completed in the newly founded town of Siri in the first decade of the 14th century.[10] The choice of Siri for his foundation can probably be attributed to strategic considerations for his military camp, being well protected on one side by the Yamuna river.[11] With the establishment of Siri, the royal citadel and the outside world came to be differentiated from each other, especially as the city grew into a powerful political centre famed and glorified throughout India and the Islamic world.

The Tughluq-founded urban centres (see figure 2) of the later 14th century also consisted of two distinct areas. One was the well-protected seat of power, normally including a strongly fortified citadel, the palaces of the sultan and his harem, and residences of the courtiers. The second was the settlement of the working population in rural or suburban habitats. This bipartite urban scheme can already be found at Rai Pithora, but is even more clearly evident at Siri, Tughluqabad, and Firuzabad. Timur describes the arrangement in his autobiography:

"I took a ride around the cities (of Delhi). Siri is a round city. Its buildings are lofty, they are surrounded by fortifications built of stone and brick, and they are very strong; old Delhi also has a similar strong fort, but it is larger than that of Siri. From the fort of Siri to that of old Delhi, which is a considerable distance, there runs a strong wall built of stone and cement. The part called Jahanpanah is situated in the midst of the inhabited city. The fortifications of the three cities have 30 gates, Jahanpanah has 13 gates, seven on the south side bearing towards the east, and six on the north side bearing towards the west. Siri has seven gates, four towards the outside, and three on the inside towards Jahanpanah. The fortifications of old Delhi have 10 gates, some opening towards the exterior, and some towards the interior of the city."[12]

This description makes it clear that most of Delhi's population lived in clusters of villages outside the fortified citadel. These villages housed the artisanal classes and farmers, who formed the backbone of the urban centres' economy and prosperity. Timur's distinction between gates "towards the exterior" and "towards the interior" hints at the relationship of these outer settlements with the fortified citadel, and with the larger world beyond, and trade routes to distant lands. In times of external attacks this arrangement provided thorough protection for the seat of power, whereas the common population remained quite vulnerable.

The Delhi sultans' desire to expand the urbanized area led to the establishment of satellite urban complexes centring around the fortified citadels. Following Siri, dating to the early 14th century, came Tughluqabad and finally Firuz Shah Kotla. These royal clusters were fortified by a strong wall and protected by battlements, bastions, water bodies, heavily guarded gateways, and secret passages. The settlements of the ordinary citizens who served these aristocratic and military groups grew around these fortified townships. Realizing the strategic disadvantage of such fragmented urban spaces, Muhammad Tughluq consciously tried to connect these clusters by a city wall, thus encasing the publicly inhabited spaces. He named his new city Jahanpanah, or "Refuge of the World". Ibn Batuta describes it as follows:

"The fourth is called Jahanpanah, and is set apart for the residence of the Sultan, Muhammad Tughluq, the reigning King of India, to whose court we had come. He was the founder of it, and it was his intention, to unite these four towns within a single wall, but after building part of it, gave up the rest because of the great expense entailed in its construction."[13]

In line with growth of the urban spaces throughout, residences, shops, mosques, and administrative buildings sprang up according to public needs and desires. Homogeneous communities such as the newly converted Mongols, were confined to separate urban quarters.[14] The Sufi religious establishments or *khanqah*s were generally scattered outside the urban conglomerations. The *khanqah* of Nizamuddin Auliyya serves as an example.

Delhi's relegation of *khanqah*s to the outskirts contrasts with Muhammad Tughluq's organization of his new capital Daulatabad. This city had quarters for every class of people, including troops, *wazir*s, secretaries, judges, merchants, and craftsmen. Learned men, sheikhs, and faqirs also lived within the urban quarters. Each of these quarters was self-contained, having mosques, bazars, public baths, ovens for making breads and any other need of each community.[15]

II. Tughluq Town-Planning and Architecture: "Palaces as Instruments of Urban Policy"[16]

Each of the fortified towns of the Tughluqs – Tughluqabad, Adilabad, Jahanpanah, Firuz Shah Kotla – was deliberately planned and built on a systematic grid. These fortified towns were founded to achieve the seemingly contradictory aims of suzerainty over an alien country, and the Tughluqs' desire for integration into their new homeland. This twofold motive might be the reason why the towns of the

3

Tughluqabad, ruins of the inner palace complex with a small pond with water channels and fountain in one of the inner chambers.
Photograph: Jutta Jain.

Tughluqs resemble strongholds with precisely planned, well laid-out, and expansive palace complexes within a fortified township.

Despite their display of strength, these centres reflected the precariously feeble situation of the Tughluq sultanate: the permanent danger of attack from within or beyond its borders made fortification of the royal court imperative. The defensive arrangement usually consisted of quasi-concentric circles of buttressed fortifications, the outer wall protecting the entire fort, the inner wall the royal residences, and within these, the personal chambers of the ruler again separately protected. The private area was usually self-contained with grain-storage facilities and wells, stepwells, and water tanks, and these were secured by strong gates leading to the heavily guarded citadel.

Tughluqabad (figures 3 and 4)

Called by some the third city of Delhi, Tughluqabad was founded by Sultan Ghiyath al-Din Tughluq as his new capital in 1321, during his first year on the throne. Completed by 1323, it served as capital for only a few years. Considering the short span of Ghiyath al-Din's reign, his building activity was enormous, ranging from the town of

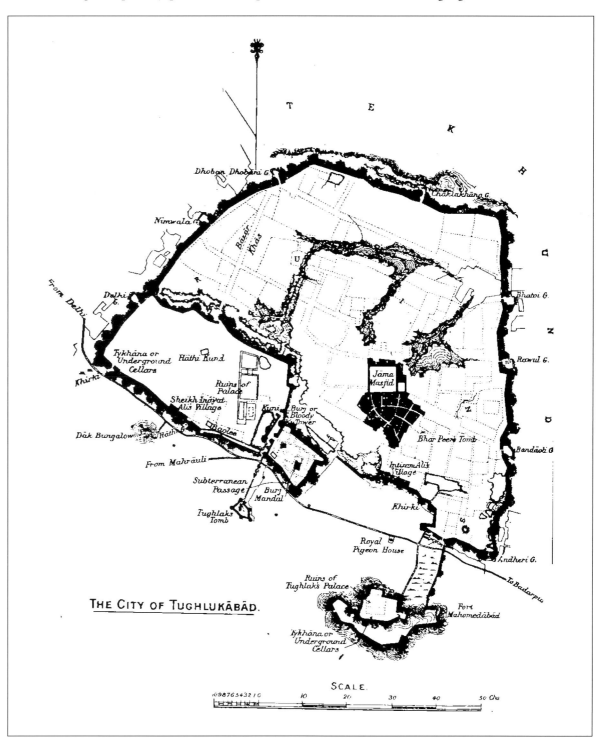

THE CITY OF TUGHLUKĀBĀD.

4

The city of Tughluqabad, reproduced from Gordon Hearn, *The Seven Cities of Delhi*, Calcutta, 1928.

5

Bijay Mandal (circa 1343),
palace buildings of Muhammad
Tughluq on the hilltop.
Photograph: Julian Jain.

6

Begumpuri Masjid (circa 1343),
congregational courtyard.
Photograph: Tanmaya Tathagat.

7

Hauz Khas complex, college building (circa 1352) of two-storeyed and domed pillared halls, with projecting balconies, built on the northern and western side of Hauz Khas lake.
Photograph: Jutta Jain.

8

Kotla Firuz Shah, the palace of Firuz Shah (circa 1354), view of the pyramidal structure with the Ashokan pillar on top.
Photograph: Tanmaya Tathagat.

Tughluqabad, to the Persianate mausoleum of Rukn-i-Alam in Multan, to his own tomb adjacent to Tughluqabad.

Tughluqabad was built on an irregular, rocky hill of massive stone-blocks, surrounded on one side by an expansive artificial body of water. The palace complex was protected by a sturdy internal wall, parts of which still exist today. An underground arched passage led from the private chambers to the sultan's own well-fortified mausoleum.[17] Ibn Batuta mentions that the city walls had in-built grain storage silos, indicating the need to safeguard the royal enclave, and the fort's citizenry. The meticulously planned geometric grid of roads with a mosque at the centre testifies to a maturity in town-planning practices.

Adilabad – Jahanpanah – Daulatabad

Adilabad was built as a subsidiary fort to Tughluqabad by Ghiyath al-Din's son Muhammad, probably shortly after Tughluqabad. Since Muhammad – like many sultans before and after him – was often out on military campaigns, Adilabad was a temporary abode.[18] He is also credited with founding Daulatabad in 1328. This was his second capital at the site of ancient Deogiri in the western Deccan, from where he attempted to establish his supremacy over southern India. This forced relocation of the capital caused resistance among many of Delhi's courtiers and townspeople. Despite this unsuccessful adventure, along with numerous and costly military campaigns, his architectural activities were substantial. He founded Jahanpanah with its expansive palace complex. From this centre only the Bijay Mandal (1343) (figure 5) and the majestic congregational mosque known as the Begumpuri Masjid (1343) remain (figures 1 and 6).

Fattahabad – Hisar Firuzah – Firuzabad

After Muhammad's sudden death during a campaign in Thatta in Sindh, his nephew Firuz Shah was crowned sultan by the leading aristocrats in 1351.[19] He founded his first town at Fattahabad in the same year, before even being formally crowned, on the spot where he witnessed his son's birth.

Firuzabad, the new town he founded in 1354, 11 kilometres to the northeast of Jahanpanah, may be considered his most important architectural achievement. Its remarkable location far north of "old Delhi" on the banks of the Yamuna was an urbanizing pattern followed by later rulers such as Shah Jahan,

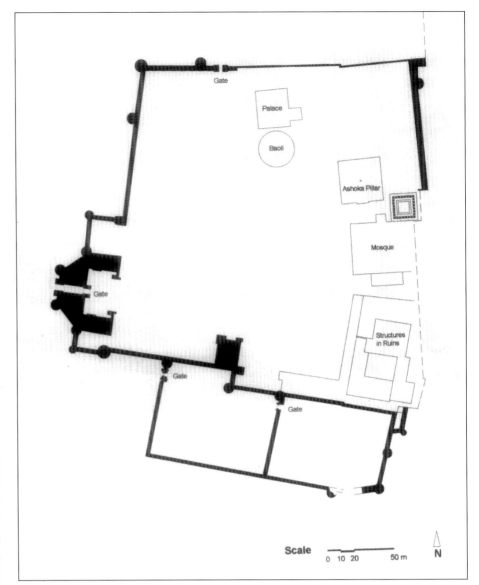

9

Plan of Kotla Firuz Shah, based on an original map of Archaeological Survey of India. Drawing by Julian Jain.

10

Khirki Mosque (circa 1352–54), view of the aisles. Photograph: Tanmaya Tathagat.

11

Khirki Mosque, view of the western face showing detail of the lower portion of one of the tapering towers with stellate plan. At the four corners watchtowers were added in keeping with the defensive vocabulary.
Photograph: Tanmaya Tathagat.

12

Khirki Mosque, the masterly conceptualized notion of space and depth is achieved by the simplicity of the arched aisles, courtyards, the plain massive pillars of roughly hewn stone blocks, and domes that are placed by simple masonry work.
Photograph: Tanmaya Tathagat.

who founded Shahjahanabad north of Firuzabad (see figure 2).

Based on the towns built by his two predecessors, Firuzabad included an inner enclosure known as Firuz Shah Kotla (figure 9) with the royal palaces, a citadel, and other private structures. Outside this enclosure were the public edifices, including the Hall for Public Audience, baths, tanks, staff and army quarters, stables, and royal gardens. Its stepwell (1354) is a harmonious rendering of functionality and architectural expression – a recreational abode with open-pillared *chattri*-like pavilions and two underground storeys of rooms opening into the well. The centre of the royal enclave was occupied by the main congregational mosque, supposedly accommodating more than a thousand people. In 1367, taking precedent from the Qutbi Mosque's iron pillar, Firuz Shah relocated an Ashokan pillar to Firuz Shah Kotla with great effort of manpower and technical logistics. He had the pillar erected in a specially designed pyramid-like structure, as if the pillar served as the towering pinnacle of his citadel (figure 8).[20]

In 1356 he founded Hisar Firuzah 130 kilometres northwest of Delhi. Although situated in a rather arid zone, this settlement (previously known as Hissar) was a traditional trading post of great economic importance, serving as the entry point for many caravans from West Asia into India. The new town was planned to supply traders, travellers, caravans, and the public at large with affordable housing and water. The town had a buttressed fort with a splendid palace "which had no equal in the world".[21] The historian Afif described in detail how the palace was rendered inaccessible by means of a complex network of narrow and dark passages.[22]

Firuz Shah's desire to improve agricultural production led him to construct two artificial waterways into the town from the Yamuna and the Sutlej rivers.[23] For two-and-a-half years Firuz Shah witnessed the construction of the town, complete with civic amenities such as canals, tanks, stepwells, gardens, and horticultural plantations. He perfected his uncle Muhammad's *satpula* (c. 1340) or seven-arched bridge in Jahanpanah, which, even in its slightly ruinous state today, is a grandiose structure. These measures brought prosperity to the region: "Previous to this time there had been an autumn harvest, but the spring harvest failed, because wheat would not grow without water. After the canals had been dug, both harvests came to maturity."[24] The Khirki Mosque (circa 1352–54) (figures 10–12) with latticed windows that gave the mosque its name, is a unique building, the stark austerity of the recessed parallel outlines around the arch being its unmistakable hallmark.

Finally, the peak architectural achievements of Firuz Shah include his two-storeyed madrasa, with arched colonnades and projecting balcony windows. This complex of 1388 also includes his tomb, with its magnificent dome construction, overlooking the Hauz Khas (figure 7). The mausoleum of Khan-i Jahan Tilangani in Nizamuddin, dating to 1368, also evinces elaborate faceted dome construction.

Conclusion

Austerity and functionality were the hallmarks of building under the Tughluqs. Architectural form dominated, with virtually no surface decoration. Very little coloured tile, stucco work, or carved stone work was used in their buildings.

It is noteworthy that, despite the turmoil of the early 14th century, the Tughluq sultans boasted such great achievements in town-planning and architecture. The Tughluqs are unique in the medieval age for their dedication to building. Despite a constantly changing political climate, often leading to precarious circumstances, the Tughluq sultans continued to be ambitious in their architectural programmes, not only commemorating their own military successes, but also engaging in more complex and daring processes of building civic institutions.

ACKNOWLEDGEMENTS

I would like to acknowledge the support of the following in writing this article: Dr K.K. Sharma of the National Museum, New Delhi, the staff of the Drawing, Photography, and Library sections of the Archaeological Survey of India, the staff of the library of the India International Centre, New Delhi. I also thank my daughter Saskya for editing, my son Julian for drawings and photography, and my husband Jyotindra for discussing the concept.

NOTES

1. Catherine Asher, *Architecture of Mughal India*, Cambridge, 1992, p. 6.

2. See note 8. Historians differ on the true identity of this Turkic tribe. Some quote Marco Polo, who describes the Qaraunahs as people of mixed origin, most probably of Turkic-Indian blood. One scholar, Sir Wolseley Haig, identifies Tughluq as "Taghlik", a tribe of Turks who still live in Khotan, quoted in *A Comprehensive History of India*, vol V: *The Delhi Sultanate AD 1206–1526*, eds. Mohammad Habib and Khaliq Ahmad Nizami, New Delhi, 1970, p. 52.

3. Though the cognomen Tughluq was attached to the personal names of only the first two emperors, Ghiyath al-Din and Muhammad Shah, for the sake of classification, modern historians clubbed all their successors as the "Tughluq dynasty".

4. Amir Khusrau (*Tughluqnama*, ed. S.H. Faridabadi, trans. S. Hushami, Hyderabad, 1933, p. 138) mentions: "Thy name was Tughluq Ghazi, the revered one. The Mongol chief too at that time had the same name, Tughluq."

5. H.M. Elliot and John Dowson, eds., *The History of India as told by its own Historians*, vol. III, reprint Allahabad, n.d., p. 382.

6. Agha Mahdi Husain, *Tughluq Dynasty*, New Delhi, 1976, p. 320.

7. Amir Khusrau, *Qiranu's-Sadain*, quoted in S.A.A. Rizvi "Socio-Religious Dimensions of Amir Khusrau's Delhi" in *Life, Times and Works of Amir Khusrau*, New Delhi, 1976, p. 3.

8. Ibn Batuta, *Rihla: The Travels in Asia and Africa*, trans. H.A. Gibb, New York, 1928, p. 618. Other Arab travellers during the 14th century describe Delhi as consisting of as many as 21 urban centres, which were grouped together, each one having a separate name. See Shaikh Abu Bakr at Khallal al-Bazze al Kufi, quoted from: W.H. Siddiqi, "The Discovery of Architectural Remains of a Pre-Mughal Terraced Garden at New Delhi", in *Archaeology and History. Essays in Memory of Shri A. Ghosh*, eds. B.M. Pande and B.D. Chattopadhyaya, Delhi, 1987, p. 574. I am grateful to Rewa Dayal for pointing out this essay to me.

9. *Tarikh-i Firuz Shahi* by Shams-i Siraj Afif, in: Elliot and Dowson, eds., *The History of India...*, vol. III, p. 303.

10. *The Delhi Sultanate* (see note 2), p. 329.

11. Ibid., p. 338.

12. *Malfuzat-i Timuri*, in Elliot and Dowson, eds., *The History of India...*, vol. III, p. 447.

13. Ibn Batuta, *Rihla*, pp. 619–20.

14. *Tarikh-i Firuz Shahi*, p. 219.

15. Shahabuddin Al'Umari, *Masalik ul-Absar Fi Mamalik ul Amsar*, trans. Otto Spies, in *Muslim University Journal Aligarh*, quoted in Rizvi (see note 7), pp. 18–19.

16. This phrase is taken from Anthony Welch and Howard Crane, "The Tughluqs: Master Builders of the Delhi Sultanate", in *Muqarnas*, New Haven and London, 1983, vol. I, p. 124.

17. Termed by Welch and Crane ("The Tughluqs", p. 128) as a "tomb-fort functioning as military refuge as well as royal necropolis".

18. He called his new residence Adilabad since he considered himself to be "*adil*" meaning "just", and occasionally this word is added to his own given name, e.g. Badauni calls the Sultan Muhammad Adil, as quoted in *Muntakhabaa't Tawarikh* quoted from Husain, *Tughluq Dynasty*, p. 56.

19. *Tarikh-i Firuz Shahi*, p. 283.

20. *Sirat-i Firuz Shahi* gives a full and detailed description of how this pillar was removed from its old site and re-erected at Kotla Firuz Shah in the specially constructed pyramid-like foundation. Quoted from Welch and Crane, "The Tughluqs", p. 164.

21. *Tarikh-i Firuz Shahi*, p. 299: "during the hot season travellers who came from Irak and Khurasan had to pay as much as four *jitals* for a pitcher full (of water). So the Sultan resolved to build a city being filled with hope that if he built a town for the benefit of Musulmans, God would provide it with water."

22. Ibid.: "This central apartment under the palace was very dark, and the passages narrow, so that if the attendants did not guide the visitor he would never be able to find his way out."

23. Ibid.

24. Ibid.

Abha Narain Lambah

The Sharqis of Jaunpur: Inheritors of the Tughluq Legacy

Of all the sultanates, the buildings of Jaunpur in eastern Uttar Pradesh represent the culmination of imperial Tughluq architecture. The Tughluqs' militaristic style, with its robust battered walls and corner buttresses, was formulated during the reign of Ghiyath al-Din Tughluq (r. 1320–25) and refined in the reign of Firuz Shah (r. 1351–88), the dynasty's most prolific builder. The monumental mosques of Jaunpur embody the zenith of this military aesthetic.

Located 60 kilometres east of Varanasi, Jaunpur is today a rather obscure town better known for its attar (scented oils) than its architectural legacy. During the 15th and 16th centuries, however, it was famous as "Shiraz-e-Hind" (the Shiraz of India), an intellectual capital renowned for its scholars, craftsmen, religious leaders, and madrasas with Sher Shah Sur being among the famous alumni.

Much of Jaunpur's pre-Islamic history was linked with Varanasi. In the early 1190s, the armies of Salar Masand Ghazi, nephew of Muhammad Ghuri, plundered across the rich riverine territories of the Gangetic plains, reached the gates of Benares,[1] and destroyed the temples of nearby Zafarabad, annexing the area to their territorial holdings farther west. The only remnants of 14th-century Islamic construction are a fort within which is a mosque built by Ibrahim Naib Barbak in 1376 (figure 2).

In 1360, Firuz Shah Tughluq founded Jaunpur near an already existing town in the area, thereby extending its urbanization. He named his city after his uncle, the preceding Tughluq sultan, Malik Juna or Muhammad (r. 1325–51).[2] The founding of the city was not completely peaceful, accompanied as it was with desecration of the temples of the existing settlement. These older buildings provided ready construction material such as stone columns, and also served religio-political propagandistic purposes.[3] Firuz Shah returned to Delhi the following winter, appointing Zafar Khan as governor of his new city. Firuz Shah's reign that was characterized by extensive patronage of urban centres, mosques, canals, gardens, and many more monumental projects, ended with his death on October 23, 1388, bringing on great instability for the Tughluq sultanate and internecine struggles over accession to the throne. During these years of Tughluq decline, Khwaja Jahan Malik Sarwar was the governor of Jaunpur. Malik Sarwar had risen from the position of one of many eunuchs in the service of Sultan Muhammad Tughluq, to Khwaja Sara or chief eunuch, and was ultimately deputed to Jaunpur with the title Malik al-Sharq (Governor of the East). With the weakening of central authority, in 1394 Malik Sarwar seized the opportunity to sever ties with his overlords and declare himself the ruler.

1
Detail of carved stone screens,
Atala Mosque.
Photograph: Ravi Kapoor.

Malik Sarwar had adopted Malik Vazir, the son of a Hindu named Karanphul, and a slave boy and water-bearer of Firuz Shah. Malik Sarwar declared the boy his successor. Finally, after the invasion of Timur in 1398, Malik Vazir declared himself independent sultan of Jaunpur as Mubarak Shah. Retaining the title bestowed on his adoptive father by the Tughluq sultans, Mubarak Shah and his successors assumed Sharqi as their dynastic name. Mubarak Shah Sharqi was succeeded by his brother Shams al-Din Ibrahim (r. 1402–36), the greatest of the Sharqi sultans. During Ibrahim's reign of over three decades, Jaunpur rose to be a premier centre for literary, religious, and architectural pursuits. Through the reigns of the next three sultans, Mahmud Shah ibn Ibrahim (r. 1436–58), Bhikan Khan Muhammad Shah (r. 1458), and Husain Shah ibn Mahmud Shah (r. 1458–83, d. 1505), until the Lodi conquest of Jaunpur, the city received royal architectural patronage in its own right. The Atala Mosque, the Congregational Mosque, the Jhanjri Mosque, Khalis Mukhlis, and Lal Darwaza all date to this period.

In a sense, it was Timur's plunder of Delhi in the late 14th century that gave an impetus to the rise of Jaunpur's stature as a city of architectural and academic refinement. Scholars, artists, master-craftsmen, and building artisans fleeing Delhi and the fate of being carried away as Timur's prisoners or forced to work at sites in Iran and Central Asia,[4] sought refuge in Jaunpur. A new interpretation of Tughluq architectural elements led to the emergence of the style distinctive to Jaunpur. Indeed, it is likely that many craftsmen trained in Delhi's imperial Tughluq style were employed in the construction of Jaunpur's mosques.[5] Jaunpur shared much with Tughluq Delhi (figure 3), including a solid, militaristic vocabulary devoid of excessive ornament, with corner buttresses, battered walls of stone masonry, and monumental gateways.

The Jaunpur Sharqi mosques were arranged around a central *sahn* (courtyard) bordered by colonnaded cloisters. Each boasted three monumental entrance gateways on the north, east, and south perimeter walls, with recessed arches and battered profiles. The fourth and largest gateway was placed at the centre of the western *liwan* (prayer area) facade, marking the central axis of the qibla. The Atala Mosque's corner turrets hearken to Delhi's Khirki Mosque (mid-14th century), while the Congregational Mosque's arch-bearing lintels can be traced to Ghiyath al-Din's tomb at Tughluqabad.

The evolution of the Sharqi structural systems is reflective of their chronology. The Atala Mosque used trabeate columns and beams making up the structural system of the cloisters. The numerous masons' marks on the stones led R. Nath to theorize that a Hindu architect supervised the construction (figure 4).[6] As Jaunpur's structural system evolved, however, later mosques used more arcuated systems and developed structural vaulting.

The temple of Atala Devi became the site of the first royal Sharqi mosque, the Atala Mosque. Construction began in 1408 under Ibrahim Sharqi, atop foundations laid during the time of Firuz Shah Tughluq.[7] The building is planned around a 54-metre-square courtyard, bordered by aisles on three sides. Its *liwan* along the conventional western wall or *qibla* measured 11 x 10 metres inside and is roofed by a hemispherical dome approximately 17 metres high, but not visible from the courtyard. The lofty stone portal, measuring 23 metres in height and nearly 17 metres in width at its base, screens the dome (figure 5). The portal in turn acts as an *iwan* and is echoed in the smaller entrance portals on the north, east, and

2

The mosque of Ibrahim Naib Barbak (1376) with a stone "lat" in its forecourt is framed by flanking cloisters of stone colonnades with pre-Islamic forms, indicating the recycling of building material from an earlier settlement.
Photograph: Ravi Kapoor.

3

The corner buttresses seen
earlier in the Khirki Mosque,
Delhi became the hallmark of
Sharqi architecture.
Photograph: Tanmaya Tathagat.

4

Stone columns and ornamental
brackets support a largely
trabeate construction of the
colonnades around the central
sahn, Atala Mosque.
Photograph: Ravi Kapoor.

5

View of the towering *qibla iwan* along the western *liwan* of the Atala Mosque.
Photograph: Ravi Kapoor.

south sides of the mosque enclosure. The building's western exterior is solid and unadorned. Its corner bastions are more in tune with defensive fortification rather than religious architecture, but true to its militaristic Tughluq legacy (figures 3 and 8).

There are differing views on the date of the Khalis Mukhlis Mosque, also known as the Char Ungli Masjid. Fuhrer suggested that it was built prior to the Atala Mosque and Brown placed it two decades afterward. It remains unchallenged, however, that the mosque was built by Malik Khalis and Malik Mukhlis, governors under Sultan Ibrahim Shah Sharqi. They constructed it for the saint Sa'id Usman, who sought refuge in Jaunpur after being driven out of Delhi by

6

The eastern gateway of the Atala Mosque formed by exterior colonnades along the outer periphery that are occupied by shops reminiscent of medieval souks.
Photograph: Ravi Kapoor.

7

Detail of the monumental arched gateway of the western *liwan* of the Atala Mosque.
Photograph: Ravi Kapoor.

Timur. The building reputedly occupies the site of a 12th-century temple patronized by Vijayachandra of Kanauj.

The Lal Darwaza Mosque of 1450 was built on a more modest scale than its precursors. It served as a private mosque within the palace complex of Bibi Raja, the queen of Mahmud Shah Sharqi (r. 1440–58), reserved for the use of the women of the royal household. The screened upper area was the zenana, which was placed in a central position next to the nave. Unlike other mosque zenanas, this compartment was not confined to the side wings, suggesting the influence of the queen. The mosque supposedly occupies the site of yet another 12th-century temple by Vijayachandra.[8]

Although heavily reliant on their Tughluq predecessors, the Jaunpur Sharqis' ambitious constructions did surpass them in concept and execution, as well as scale and sophistication. The Atala Mosque was a bold experiment. As a starting point, it relied on the Begumpuri Mosque's configuration of the central courtyard on an elevated platform, accessed by a flight of steps. The Atala Mosque, however,

dispensed with the high plinth and flight of steps and instead introduced a row of cells in its outer periphery facing the street outside (figure 6). The modern shops along the ground level are consistent with the souks of the 15th century. Its monumental portals of sloping towers flanking massive arches served as *iwans* (monumental niche used as a framing device). These portals became the signature of Sharqi royal mosques (figure 7). Indeed, the already formidable height of the Atala gateways was increased in the ambitious Congregational Mosque. The scale and monumentality of Jaunpur's mosques towered over Delhi's Kalan, Begumpuri, and Khirki mosques (figure 3), which were Jaunpur's Tughluq predecessors.

Of all the mosques of Jaunpur, the Jhanjri Mosque shows the finest detailing and is remarkable for the sheer delicacy of ornament (figure 9). Shifting from the more solid, rugged handsomeness of the earlier mosques, it reveals a delicate, almost feminine aesthetic. The mosque was built by Ibrahim Shah Sharqi in 1430 on the site of the riverside temple of Muktaghat, in honour of the saint Hazrat Sa'id Sadr Jahan Ajmali. The mosque was subjected to the

8

The rear of the western *liwan* of the Atala Mosque characterized by solid masonry and corner buttresses. Photograph: Ravi Kapoor.

onslaught of the vandalizing armies of Sikander Lodi[9] and only the western portal survives as a witness of its former glory. While the Atala and other earlier mosques are spartan in decoration, the Jhanjri Mosque revels in a highly evolved aesthetic sensibility. The building derives its name from *jhanjar* or screen, likely a reference to the rich architectural treatment and finely carved stone screens spanning the massive arch of the western portal (figure 10). The Jhanjri Mosque's shift to ornamentation has been interpreted by some scholars as an indication of decadence, signalling a decline of the robust Sharqi traditions.[10] I would argue

9

Jhanjri Mosque – only the western portal survives. This was substantially repaired by the Archaeological Survey of India in 1992 with a near complete dismembering and anastylosis – piecing together its carved stones.
Photograph: Ravi Kapoor.

10

Detail of arch, Jhanjri Mosque.
Photograph: Ravi Kapoor.

that the shift was not indicative of imminent decline, as the Congregational Mosque, the largest and most ambitious Sharqi structure, was constructed four decades later.

Last among the Sharqi foundations, the Congregational Mosque, now known as the Bari Masjid, was completed in 1473 by Husain Shah Sharqi. Historical sources vary as to its raison d'etre. Some sources hold that the building was designed under Ibrahim Shah (though not commenced), as the sultan wished to save an old hermit, Khwaja Isa, the trouble of walking barefoot to the Khalis Mukhlis for Friday prayers. Other sources suggest, however, that the project was undertaken in order to create employment for the craftsmen of Jaunpur, who had been suffering the effects of a seven-year famine.[11]

Whatever its reason for being, the Congregational Mosque is undoubtedly the grandest of the Sharqi edifices, exhibiting an unprecedented monumentality and confidence in scale and construction.[12] An impressive flight of steps leads to the high plinth of the courtyard, with monumental gateways underscoring the grandiosity of the whole (figure 11). The *liwan* along the western perimeter measures 18 metres in depth and 77 metres in length. It is divided into five bays, with one of these carrying the zenana. The enclosing aisles on the other three sides were double-storeyed when viewed from outside the building, but single-storeyed when viewed from the *sahn* (figure 12).

The three entrance portals, one in the centre of each perimeter aisle, acted as preludes to the central portal of the *liwan*. This *qibla iwan* is 26 metres high and 23.5 metres wide at the base. The mosque basically conformed to the plans of other Sharqi mosques, with the exception of the raised plinth. However, at the Congregational Mosque such an architectural reference is in sync with the political landscape as it was during the reign of Husain Shah that Jaunpur ceased to be an independent sultanate and once again entered the yoke of another Delhi-based power, the Lodis. It was unique, however, in its large vaulted halls flanking the western portals. As noted in the discussion of other Sharqi mosques, these portals evolved from Delhi's Tughluq buildings.

This impending *political* dominion by Delhi did not preclude the input of *architectural* practices from other regions. The vaulted halls flanking the monumental portal, mentioned above, provide a case in point. Looking eastward, Jaunpur's proximity to

11

The western gateway of the Congregational Mosque screening the dome behind it. Photograph: Ravi Kapoor.

12

Congregational Mosque, view of the dome on the western *liwan* screened by the monumental arched gateway. Photograph: Ravi Kapoor.

Bengal resulted in the adoption of the vault from the Adina Mosque at Pandua (1375), assimilating the form with unprecedented panache in the Congregational Mosque. Its stone vaults span 12 metres and are supported on stone ribs for centring. Over this substructure stone slabs were laid and finished with lime concrete. The overall effect was a grand vaulted space unobstructed by pillars.

It is noteworthy that the Sharqi patrons commissioned no remarkable tombs. Instead of monumental tombs, the entire royal family was buried in a modest graveyard adjoining the northern wall of the Congregational Mosque (figure 13). Ibrahim Shah, Mahmud Shah, Husain Shah and other members of the royal family were interred without any exterior sepulchre or monumental edifice, as the Sharqi rulers made a statement, even in death, of a simple life.

Sikandar Lodi besieged Jaunpur in 1480, avenging Husain Shah's earlier campaign against Delhi.[13] The Lodi forces wrought destruction on the city's Sharqi buildings, probably razing much of the secular architecture. They certainly demolished the eastern portal and aisles of the Congregational Mosque[14] and damaged the Jhanjri Mosque. Jaunpur was virtually destroyed. What had begun as Sikandar Lodi's revenge for the Sharqi campaign against Delhi resulted in the utter ruination of the Sharqi dynasty.

Here end the architectural commentaries of most historians, limiting the entire architectural debate on Jaunpur to less than a century of Sharqi rule. However, though largely unsung, over the next four centuries Jaunpur continued its architectural development, borrowing at times from imperial styles, tempered by geographical factors and at other times influencing even the imperial styles of Lodi Delhi and Sher Shah Sur's architecture in Narnaul.

In subsequent decades, as the Lodis exerted control over Jaunpur, they carried Jaunpuri craftsmen to Delhi to work on the imperial Lodi tombs. These craftsmen conveyed the Sharqi aesthetic and architectural concepts, influencing Lodi tomb design and architectural ornament. An example is Sikandar Lodi's own Bada Gumbad.[15] It is ironic that the only notable structures commissioned in Jaunpur by the Lodis were funerary structures. This patronage of funereal architecture was in keeping with the Lodis, who were among the most prolific tomb builders of their time.

The most eminent among the post-Sharqi tombs in Jaunpur is the tomb of Faqir Firuz Shah, located in the Sipah Muhalla (figure 14). Built of brick with lime plaster, the tomb is a square structure on the outside with an octagonal interior. An octagonal drum rises atop the parapet, surmounted by a dome. The latter's pinnacle harkens to many examples of Suri

13

The royal cemetery adjoining the northern wall of the Congregational Mosque. Photograph: Ravi Kapoor.

14

The tomb of Faqir Firuz Shah
– a protected monument.
Photograph: Ravi Kapoor.

15

The hauntingly beautiful
Kalichkhan ka Maqbara lies
derelict and unprotected along
the riverbank.
Photograph: Ravi Kapoor.

16

The reconstructed eastern
gateway of the Congregational
Mosque.
Photograph: Ravi Kapoor.

architecture. Blue encaustic tile work is used for decoration. The merlon design on the parapet is traced to Sharqi mosques. Another notable mausoleum is the Kalichkhan ka Maqbara, picturesquely sited along the south bank of the Gomti and built on a Baghdadi plan – square-chamfered at the corners to create an octagonal form (figure 15).

Jaunpur was still a renowned centre of learning during the youth of Sher Shah Sur, who studied in one of Jaunpur's numerous madrasas. When Sher Shah occupied the Delhi throne (r. 1540–45), he established a mint at Jaunpur and trade links continued with the mint town of Narnaul. Jaunpur continued to be an important holding under Munim Khan during Akbar's reign (1556–1605). Mughal-period constructions include a bridge over the Gomti river and a distinctive style of mosque architecture.[16] Domestic architecture of the 17th, 18th, and 19th centuries had palpable affinities with nearby Awadh.

Jaunpur's Sharqi mosques are protected national monuments. However, in 1928–29 negotiations between the Archaeological Survey of India (ASI) and the mosques' *imam*s failed to reach an agreement. Since then, government involvement has been minimal in the maintenance of the Congregational Mosque, the Lal Darwaza Mosque, and the Atala Mosque, all under active worship.[17] Instead, the ASI office in Jaunpur has busied itself with repair work on secular structures such as the fort,[18] the Gomti bridge, and the disused Jhanjri Mosque.[19]

In 1977, nearly 500 years after the Congregational Mosque's east aisles and portal were destroyed by Sikandar Lodi, a quiet, grassroots initiative began to restore and reconstruct the damaged portal.[20] Under the guidance of the Congregational Mosque's *imam*, Maulana Zafar Ahmad Siddiqi, local craftsmen with no formal education worked on the ambitious reconstruction of the main eastern portal. Employing local stone, lime mortar, and hand-held tools, the craftsmen have rebuilt the portal and its dome, largely with the same technology and methods available to Sharqi craftsmen five centuries ago (figure 16).

This public conservation effort has lasted 28 years,[21] and has been entirely funded and managed by the local community. Due to the absence of documentation of the east portal and aisles before their destruction in the 15th century, the portal was reconstructed using the extant two portals as models. This example of public involvement in the conservation of a historical monument in a small *mufassil* town, without the support of formally trained engineers, archaeologists, or conservation professionals, throws open a new perspective on historic conservation and public involvement in living religious monuments. Such public intervention rekindles debates over authenticity and the significance of historic preservation, challenging international charters and accepted conservation philosophies.

ACKNOWLEDGEMENT

The author is grateful to Ravi Kapoor for his ready cooperation and enthusiastic support in making a special trip to Jaunpur to take the photographs for this article.

NOTES

1. *Mirat al Asar* and *Tawarikh Minimi* referred to in A. Fuhrer and W. Smith, "The Sharqi Architecture of Jaunpur with notes on Zafarabad, Sahet-Mahet and other places in the North Western Provinces and Oudh", Archaeological Survey of India, New Delhi, 1994 (first published 1889).

2. Fuhrer suggests that this was however, not the first tryst of Firuz with the city of Jaunpur, for in 1355, when he had marched against Haji Ilias of Lakhnauti up to Benares, he had probably ventured through this territory. However, his concerns were other than mere warfare when he revisited this area five years later, for while he camped at the banks of the Gomti in the heavy monsoon rains, he was accompanied by his first-born, the seven-year-old Prince Fath Khan who died fifteen years later leaving his father inconsolable. A father's concern for his child's training was perhaps paramount in the mind of this proud warrior king and he decided to lay the foundations of a new city that would be a centre of education and excellence, taking care to settle people of learning and wealth in his new city.

3. According to the 19th-century writings of A. Fuhrer, "One morning in April 1360, Firoz rode over to Zafarabad, attended by Jayachandra, a Rajput prince of the Gaharwar clan. At the end of his journey he found a thriving town extending for some miles along the northern bank of the Gomti and boasting four large temples, two at least conspicuous for size and costliness, a palace and a tank of cut stone. The two chief temples first attracted the king's notice but though the people looked on and worked patiently while he threw down the temple Karalavira, cast upon a mound on its site and built on it and round it a fort of stones brought from the ruined temples of Zafarabad, an attempt to desecrate the temple of Ataladevi met with so fierce a resistance that after much bloodshed, Firuz was compelled to make a compromise and give a written undertaking that the temples should be left untouched and Hindu worship tolerated, stipulating only that the temple of Ataladevi be left unrestored and perhaps unused." See Fuhrer and Smith (see note 1).

4. Surendra Sahai, *Indian Architecture: Islamic Period 1192–1857*, Prakash Books, New Delhi, 2004, p. 64.

5. According to Percy Brown, "There must therefore have been engaged in the production of the Atala mosque, a number of workmen trained in the traditions of the imperial style at Delhi." See Percy Brown, *Indian Architecture (Islamic Period)*, D.B. Taraporevala Sons & Co., Bombay, 1956, p. 43.

6. R. Nath, *History of Sultanate Architecture,* Abhinav Publications, New Delhi, 1978, p. 100.

7. R. Nath (see note 6) refers to a stone inscription in Devanagiri on the east gate, recording its commencement in the reign of Firuz Shah Tughluq by Khwaja Kamal Khan Jehan in 1376 with a Hindu architect Padum, son of architect Visai.

8. A stone inscription in Devanagiri records, "In the Samvat year 1225, on the 5th day of the dark fortnight of the month Chaitra, on Wednesday, during the reign of the fortunate Vijayachandra Deva, the venerable Bhuvibhushana."

9. Fuhrer and Smith, p. 41.

10. Brown (see note 5) states, "It also conveys that the builders were not so much concerned in its construction or the proportion of its parts, but were more interested in the plastic treatment of its surfaces…" and "…it might be presumed that the Jhangiri Masjid was an instance of that elegance without strength which foretells an approaching decline."

11. "The foundation of the building was laid in A.H. 842 or 1438 A.D. but it was not raised above the level of the ground in 844, when the king died as Khairuddin mentions. It is said that the date of completion of the masjid was found in the words 'Masjid Jami usk Sharqq' engraved on the eastern gate. This would

fix the date at 1448 A.D. as the reign of Mahmud Shah. Accordingly, some accounts state the inscription was 'Al Masjid Jami us Sharqi' making the date 1473 A.D. or A.H. 883, just before the attack of Sikander Lodi." Fuhrer and Smith.

12. In the words of A. Fuhrer, "As you look down from the upper chambers into the central hall of the Jami Masjid, when, as the evening draws on, the deepening gloom and the dimmer distance make you feel as standing in a noble shrine of a more familiar faith, the voice of some worshipper below, echoing through the vaults, carries you back to a time when, through the same lattice, some queen looked down on king and nobles gleaming in the light of pendant lamps, with the gold and jewels of an Eastern court, as they listened to the words of some saintly philosopher seated on that very pulpit." See Fuhrer and Smith, p. 63.

13. Percy Brown states, "Had not the Delhi Sultan Sikandar Lodi at the close of the 15th century, shown his implacable enmity towards the last of the Sharqi kings of Jaunpur by ruthlessly destroying and mutilating the monuments of that dynasty, its buildings would have provided a provincial manifestation of Indo-Islamic architecture of more than ordinary interest."

14. W. Smith, in his architectural description of Jami Masjid in the 19th century records that the upper floor of the double storeyed cloisters of Jami were pulled down by Sikandar Lodi, and on the subject of the demolished east entrance of the Jami Masjid clarifies, "the section through the courtyard – Plate LI, fig. 2 shows the east entrance which is in the same dismantled condition as it was left by Sikandar Lodi, and not, as asserted by some, 'thrown down by Englishmen in order to repair the station roads'." Fuhrer and Smith, p. 53.

While it is an accepted fact corroborated by Fuhrer, Brown, Grover and other architectural historians that the Jami Masjid was destroyed as an act of war by the Lodis (perhaps mistaking the militaristic architecture for a fortress or if the royal family had taken refuge there), the only author who hotly contests this fact is R. Nath, who states, "There is no truth in the statement that Sikandar Lodi demolished their buildings." This however, seems a rather subjective remark unsubstantiated by evidence, especially in the light of the fact that he seems to have been rather disparaging of the entire epoch of Sharqi architecture in general, literally writing off the architecture of the Sharqis in this most biased statement, "they introduced no new feature in their mosque". Especially disparaging are his comments, "The barrel vault of the Jami Masjid is an ugly and haphazard experiment which obviously miscarried. It spoiled the charm of the facade", and "that the Sharqis never thought of providing their people with a bridge across the Gomti and they never raised magnificent tombs to perpetuate their memory shows that they had little architectural taste". These are rather subjective statements, given that the structural and architectural innovations of the Sharqis is widely acknowledged. See Nath (see note 6), p. 106.

15. "... the Afghan-descended Lodi dynasty (1451–1526) made rigorous efforts to revive the city's status. They vanquished their enemies, the Sharqis of Jaunpur, and soon afterward commenced extensive building in Delhi itself. Certain motifs on Lodi buildings are identical to those seen earlier only in Jaunpur. This is the case, for example, with engaged colonettes embellished with an interwoven pattern on the Bara Gumbad.... This suggests that artists were taken to Delhi from Jaunpur, until then considered the cultural center of Islamic India, in an attempt to revive the prestige of the traditional capital". Catherine Asher, *Architecture of Mughal India,* Cambridge, 1992, p. 11.

16. The masjid of Hakim Sultan Muhammad dated 1570, and the masjid of Nawab Mohsin Khan in Hammam Darwaza dated 1567 are two Akbarid period mosques with dated inscriptions, and another masjid, of Shah Kabir, was built in 1583, also during the reign of Akbar.

17. Abha Narain, unpublished thesis, "Religious Islamic Architecture of Jaunpur & Public Involvement in Conservation Intervention", School of Planning & Architecture, New Delhi, 1996, lists the following works undertaken by the ASI referring to the Annual Reports of the Archaeological Survey of India between 1926 and 1990:

1926–27 Cleaning of the land around Jhanjri Masjid. Fencing off an area of 1000 sq. yards (836 sq. m).

1927–28 Efforts to get Mutwallis of Sharqi mosques to sign agreement fail.

1928–29 No repairs at Jami, Atala, Lal Darwaza due to failure of agreement.

1950s Only repairs and maintenance of Shahi Pul and Fort secular structures.

1960s Kankar lime concrete apron laid around Jhanjri Mosque, conductor for lightning. Kankar lime repair of Khalis Mukhlis Masjid. Rauza of Firuz Shah cleaned, fenced.

1965–66 Layer of dead lime concrete over Khalis Mukhlis terrace scraped, new coat added.

1970s Repair, maintenance, lime pointing, removal of vegetation etc. of Jhanjri and Khalis Mukhlis.

1980s M.S. grills installed in Char Ungli, Jhanjri, and Shah Firuz ka Maqbara.

1990s Structural consolidation of Char Ungli supporting piers, propping of vaults, domes. Arch of Jhanjri being carefully dismantled, documented, and replicated.

18. *Indian Archaeology – A Review, 1973–74,* Archaeological Survey of India, New Delhi, 1979.

19. In 1994 and 1995, the Jaunpur office of the Archaeological Survey of India, under the Patna Circle carried out a dismembering and re-piecing together of the arched stone pylon of the Jhanjri Masjid. This was documented by the author during her visit in 1994 and subsequently in 1995. Ten years later, in 2004, the author photographed the gateway pylon, fully restored.

20. The entire eastern pylon and the eastern cloisters of the Jami Masjid destroyed by Sikander Lodi continued to be in ruins until the 20th century and were documented and published as a photo-lithograph by the Calcutta office of the Survey of India in 1888.

21. In the years 1994 and 1995, this writer documented the works of the reconstruction of the eastern gateway of the Jami Masjid, being undertaken by a team of seven local *mistri*s. Though the masonry work for the entrance archway was nearly complete, the dome was not in place. Ten years later, in 2004, the author photographed the gateway with the dome erected over the drum and plaster work was yet to commence. See Narain, unpublished thesis.

1

Sher Shah's tomb, Sasaram,
Bihar, 1545.

Catherine B. Asher

Building a Legacy: Sher Shah Sur's Architecture and the Politics of Propaganda

Sher Shah Sur (r. 1538–45) rose from obscurity to become the most powerful ruler Delhi had had since the mid-14th century. He was unusual in his time, in that he lacked the respectable lineage normally associated with Indian sultans. His obscure origins were certainly to be contrasted with those of the Mughals, whom he challenged for politico-military supremacy in Hindustan. For while Sher Shah's lineage boasted nothing worthy of note, Nasir al-Din Humayun ibn Babur (r. 1530–40 and 1555) claimed matrilineal descent from the legendary Chingiz Khan, and patrilineal descent from the equally formidable Timur. As will be discussed in this essay, Sher Shah's humble origins may have had some impact on his frenetic building activity.

Sher Shah's success can be attributed to several factors. He made his bid for control from the hinterlands and hence did not appear as a threat to Humayun until it was too late. Moreover, through marriage, alliance, and loot he was able to amass extraordinary wealth. Finally, his was clearly a charismatic personality, a feature of several rulers of 16th-century north India including Babur (r. 1526–30) and the future Mughal emperor Akbar (r. 1556–1605). In addition to these factors was Sher Shah's ability to raise a massive army composed not only of Afghans but also of groups drawn from north India's diverse communities. He assured their loyalty through regular salary and consistent discipline. Sher Shah's recognition of India's multiple communities is also displayed in his coin issues, which were inscribed in both Hindi and Persian.

Although he only ruled for seven years, Sher Shah is known for his prolific and widespread architectural patronage, including buildings and public works throughout the Punjab in modern Pakistan, to Bengal as far east as Dhaka. For example, he constructed four major highways linking all of north India. The best known links Bengal to the Punjab and is known alternately as the Grand Trunk Highway – the old British name, or National Highway Number One, or Sher Shah Suri Marg in recognition of its original patron.

2

Shergarh, Bihar, 16th century.
View from fortifications to river
valley below.

He was also the builder of forts across his entire domain from the eastern part of India to its westernmost borders. Most of these forts no longer survive as they were constructed of mud, which despite their seeming fragility were effective for defensive purposes. Their walls absorbed enemy cannon, rather than exploding on impact. However, the largest of his forts were built of stone. Some were built anew, while others had been constructed previously and either partially appropriated by Sher Shah. Until he shifted his headquarters to Delhi, his base in Bihar was an ancient, naturally defended fort known as Rohtas. Sher Shah renamed it Shergarh, the official name shared by all of his fortifications. At Rohtas-Shergarh, he constructed a mosque inside the fort but it is unclear whether he built new walls or gates.

Only 22 kilometres northwest of Rohtas, another of Sher Shah's forts (still called Shergarh), is remotely yet spectacularly situated on a spur of the Kaimar range and bounded on two sides by the Durgawati river (figure 2). The fort's interior buildings evince two styles. One of these can be associated with the 14th-century Tughluq style of Delhi and Daulatabad, while the other is more in keeping with Sher Shah's own tomb in Sasaram 32 kilometres to the southwest (see figure 1). The presence of two distinct styles suggests that Sher Shah appropriated an older fort to which he made additions. Another example of a fort appropriated by Sher Shah is Delhi's Purana Qila. It was commenced by Humayun and originally known as the Din Pannah, though ultimately completed under Sher Shah. The practice of appropriating older foundations can also explain how so many structures across such a vast distance are attributable to his patronage.

Nevertheless, there are structures which were started and completed by Sher Shah. The massive Shergarh fort in western Punjab, today in Pakistan, known as Little Rohtas after his larger fort in Bihar, was built completely under his auspices (figure 3). There are at least five inscriptions on the fort's twelve entrance gates. Several of these inscriptions indicate that the fort was built in an extremely short time span between 1541/42 and 1543/44. It is probable that different groups of workers were assigned specific sections of the complex, including its walls and gates, so that the various parts of the complex were built concurrently and hence in a relatively short period of time. This was a well known building technique in the Islamic world known as *alang*.

Sher Shah also provided for his subjects' welfare by building serais, deep stepwells, and hospices for the poor. All of these charitable endeavours can be understood and justified by medieval texts on Islamic kingship, which were well known in 16th-century Islamic India. According to these texts, it is the obligation of a good ruler to provide for the subjects' welfare and security. Even Abu al-Fazl, the Mughal emperor Akbar's panegyrist, grudgingly acknowledged the great justice and fairness of their erstwhile enemy Sher Shah.

Sher Shah's desire to serve Islam, which was part of the obligations of a good sultan, can be seen in the construction of his most ornate mosque inside the Delhi citadel, today known as the Qala-i Kuhna (figure 4). This mosque makes explicit reference to the recent Islamic past of the Indian subcontinent. For example, several features such as the use of coloured stones throughout the mosque, the cusped entrance arches, and the long bands of carved inscriptions were specifically borrowed from the Alai Darwaza, Ala al-Din Khalji's early 14th-century extension to Delhi's oldest mosque (figure 5). Just as Sher Shah in his own mosque referenced the architecture of Ala al-Din, so he included regulations initially employed by Ala al-Din in his administration as well. An example is the branding of horses, a practice which ensured that horses required for service could not be counted multiple times.

I propose that Sher Shah's building programme was part of a carefully organized propagandistic campaign, designed to tout him visually as an ideal

3

Sohail Darwaza, Shergarh, known as Little Rohtas, Punjab, Pakistan,1541/42–1543/44.

4

Qala-i Kuhna Mosque in
Shergarh, today known as Purana
Qila, New Delhi, circa 1540–45.
Photograph: Tanmaya Tathagat.

5

Alai Darwaza, south extension to
Delhi's first Jami mosque,
Mehrauli, New Delhi, 1311.

Muslim sultan. However, it must be said at the outset that the three monumental tombs he had constructed – one for his grandfather, one for his father, and another for himself, all built concurrently with his public works – do not fit as well into this proposed campaign of propaganda. From this overview of his patronage, the question we must ask is why a sultan, clearly interested in promoting the self-image of a ruler concerned for his subjects, should squander resources on three enormous tombs.

In 1542/43, Sher Shah built a square-plan tomb for his grandfather, Ibrahim Sur, at Narnaul (figure 6), about 75 kilometres southwest of Delhi. Ibrahim had been an Afghan emigre horse trader and low-ranking noble in the service of the Lodi rulers (1451–1526). He was given Narnaul as his landholding.

At the time of its construction in the mid-16th century, the tomb's facade of pink and grey contrasting stone made it the most elegant and refined mausoleum in the Delhi region. Looming high above the surrounding countryside, this enormous structure dominated the older adjacent tomb of a famous saint,

Shaikh Muhammad Turk Narnauli. Since the saint's shrine had long been a site of pilgrimage, Narnaul had attracted devotees for generations. These devotees were now doubtless as awed by the monumental and imposing elegance of Ibrahim Sur's tomb, as they were spiritually affected by the saint's modest resting place immediately to the south. Buried in such close proximity to the renowned saint, Ibrahim Sur, in accordance with Islamic tradition, was imbued with the saint's *baraka* or divine essence.

Other aspects of the tomb also draw from architecture associated with saints. For example, its extremely tall platform and facades were modelled on the tomb of Khwaja Khizr in nearby Sonepat and dated to 1522–24 (figure 7). Over the entrance to Ibrahim Sur's tomb is an inscription which, while badly effaced, is still legible. The epigraph is highly unusual in that it describes the structure not only as a tomb, but also as a madrasa. This religious reference associates the tomb even more closely with that of the saint.

The interior of Ibrahim Sur's tomb is as impressive as its exterior, indeed more striking than

6

Tomb of Ibrahim Sur,
Narnaul, Haryana, 1542/43.

7

Tomb of Khwaja Khizr,
Sonepat, Haryana, 1522/24.

8

Interior, tomb of Ibrahim Sur,
Narnaul, Haryana, 1542/43.

any earlier tomb in all of India (figure 8). The *qibla* wall (oriented in the direction of Mecca) bears three prayer niches or mihrabs. Each of these mihrabs is designed differently. Such a variation creates visual imbalance in the most sacred area of the building, one which in other tombs usually has a single focal mihrab. In Ibrahim Sur's tomb, horizontal panels of Quranic verses are placed above the central and northern mihrabs, while the corresponding panel on the southern mihrab has no epigraph. Instead the panel is embellished with a series of arched niches.

While upon cursory examination the exterior also appears magnificent and perfectly crafted, close scrutiny reveals many inconsistencies in design. The spandrels of the north facade, for example, bear a continuous inlaid pattern, while those on the south facade have stellate medallions. We might ask why there is such a diversity of designs when symmetry is usually the guiding principle in tomb architecture.

As mentioned above, several inscriptions on Ibrahim Sur's tomb indicate that it was completed in 1542–43. At this very time, Sher Shah was in the midst of an extensive building campaign, one that included other tombs and public works. This intense activity sought to present Sher Shah as an ideal Muslim ruler, yet it required considerable rapidity if the message of the campaign was to be delivered immediately. The hasty construction, then, permitted attention only to the structure's overall impact, but not to minor details. It is likely that, similar to the construction of Little Rohtas in western Punjab, a number of artisans were working concurrently on the structure.

Sher Shah built the tomb over his grandfather's grave shortly after attaining the Delhi throne in 1540. This was more than 50 years after the death of Ibrahim Sur – a grandfather, by the way, he never knew. This posthumous commemoration by a descendant begs for attention, for it is unprecedented for a king to construct a tomb for a long-deceased relative. Rather, such commemoration has thus far been documented in the construction of tombs and shrines for saints. Sher Shah in effect associated the tomb of his grandfather with that of a saint in its proximity to the latter, thereby endowing it with the religious character

9

Hasan Sur's tomb, Sasaram, Bihar, circa 1538–45.

of a shrine as well. We shall see that, much in the same way, Sher Shah also imbued the tomb of his father with many trappings of a shrine.

If the tomb of Ibrahim Sur was cast as a glorified shrine, how might we interpret one of the most famous of Indo-Islamic structures, Sher Shah's own tomb in Sasaram, about 900 kilometres east of Narnaul, and that of his father Hasan Sur, also in Sasaram? Sher Shah's monumental octagonal mausoleum – at the time of its construction, the largest tomb in India – is situated in the middle of a lake (figure 1). The tomb is a three-storeyed structure whose lower level is a single, eight-sided chamber surrounded by a covered veranda. Originally, the tomb's central dome was surmounted by a single kiosk, evocative of an umbrella, a king's royal perquisite. The tomb of Hasan Sur, Sher Shah's father, is also an octagonal tomb, but smaller in scale (figure 9).

Sher Shah's tomb is dated August 16, 1545, while his father's tomb bears an inscription simply stating that it was built by Sher Shah Sultan. Since Sher Shah assumed the title Sultan in 1538, the tomb must date between that year and his death in 1545. Thus these tombs, like all other monuments constructed under Sher Shah's patronage, were raised during an intensive period of building activity lasting about seven years. The carelessly bonded stone and overall mediocre quality of construction indicate that they were built with the same haste that had resulted in the asymmetrical ornament of Ibrahim Sur's tomb. While the overall impact of these tombs is one of monumentality, close scrutiny reveals the carving to be unrefined. In addition, Sher Shah's tomb sits askew on its square plinth in order to align it in the direction of Mecca. Since artisans were fully aware of how to determine the correct orientation of buildings it is likely that the tomb sits in a pre-existing tank and on an already completed platform, originally intended for another purpose. Just as Sher Shah had appropriated and renovated older forts at Delhi and Shergarh (Bihar), his own tomb makes use of the remains of a previous construction.

Like Narnaul, Sasaram had also long been a pilgrimage site and important crossroad. High on a hill which looms over the city, is the shrine of Pir Chandan, associated with the introduction of Islam in this part of India; adjacent to the Pir's grave is an Ashokan rock-cut edict which attracted many devotees. Pir Chandan's hill thus served as an appropriate backdrop for the tombs of Sher Shah and Hasan Sur, seated in the metaphoric shade of Sasaram's oldest sacred site.

While the actual mausolea of Sher Shah and Hasan Sur are similar in appearance, their settings and, by extension, the meanings implied by these settings, are quite different. Sher Shah's tomb sits in a tank, a clear reference to al-Kausar, the heavenly fountain of spiritual rewards. This reference is specifically spelled out, for the Quranic chapter al-Kausar, or Abundance, is inscribed on the tomb's prayer niche. Thus Sher Shah constructed for himself a monument in which the entire setting was intended to represent paradise, the world of eternity.

The tomb Sher Shah built for his father, Hasan Sur, is situated in a walled, rectangular compound. His octagonal mausoleum is a smaller version of Sher Shah's, but still considerably larger than other contemporaneous tombs. Emphasizing the sacred rather than the royal, the compound recalls a saint's shrine. Contained within this walled compound is a large mosque and a madrasa, both unusual in Indian tomb complexes. Just outside this wall is a deep tank, recalling the step wells usually found at major saints' shrines, including some patronized by Sher Shah.

Besides these religious structures in the compound, certain devices on the tomb itself suggest that Sher Shah intended to cast a religious and saintly aura around the tomb complex of his father. For example, Quranic verses incised in stucco originally covered the exterior facade and interior passage of the tomb's ambulatory. On other Indian tombs of the period, only one or two Quranic verses, if any at all, appear in these locations. If historical inscriptions are carved on earlier tombs, they almost invariably appear on the exterior, while Quranic verses are usually reserved for the interior. Precisely the opposite pertains at Hasan Sur's tomb. Here, the sole historical inscription appears on the mihrab, of all places. It proclaims the patron to be Sultan Sher Shah, and also names the interred. Sher Shah's titles usually commence as Farid al-Daula wa al-Din, meaning, Farid of the state and religion. Here, however, they are reversed, placing religion first, a transposition that mirrors the reversal of religious and historical inscriptions on the tomb itself.

This inscription describes Hasan Sur as Bandagi Miyan, a phrase indicating servitude or devotion. Here it most likely refers to Hasan Sur's devotion to God since the phrase appears on the most sacred location in the entire tomb. However, this term

10

Tomb of Mubarak Khan, South Extension, New Delhi, 1481.

also may be an ironic reference to Sher Shah's respect for his father – more fictionalized than real. Thus the pious character of both father and son are elevated. Hasan Sur is endowed with saint-like qualities, and Sher Shah becomes the devoted son after his father's death that he never was during his life.

The ambulatory surrounding each of these two octagonal tombs was used for the rite of circumambulation. In India, circumambulation was performed particularly during a ceremony celebrated annually in remembrance of deceased saints. Equally appropriate for funereal architecture is the octagonal shape, likely an allusion to the eight paradises of Islamic cosmology.

Long-standing royal associations make this octagonal tomb type with a covered ambulatory appropriate for Sher Shah's tomb. But that does not explain so readily why this type was chosen for Hasan Sur's tomb as well. It is possible that Sher Shah

constructed his father's tomb in this form to imply a status that Hasan Sur, had not, in fact, ever had.

Why was Sher Shah so concerned with imbuing his own tomb and that of his low-ranking predecessors with meanings which enhanced their social status? Sher Shah's rise to power was viewed as *bi-adab,* a term indicating impropriety. For a man of his background to assume the title Sultan transcended codes of conduct established for Islamic princes. In *adab* literary sources, high birth was often cited as a prerequisite for kingship, yet Sher Shah failed to meet this requirement. The Surs were a minor Afghan tribe. Sher Shah's horse-trader grandfather had migrated to India in the late 15th century. Upon arrival, he was granted a low rank known as 40-horse and some villages near Narnaul. He died in about 1488 without rising in status. Hasan Sur, Sher Shah's father, attained a somewhat higher status when he was granted a more elevated rank and lands in the easternmost hinterlands.

Nevertheless, the family hardly belonged to the upper echelons.

Besides Sher Shah's undistinguished heritage, accounts of his character underscore an unworthy nature. One states that the young Sher Shah practised "theft and robbery", thus distressing his father. However, most contemporary writers claim it was Hasan Sur who mistreated Sher Shah, not Sher Shah who was in error. Nevertheless, the Afghan code of behaviour specified that no matter what the cause, disobedience to a father is unacceptable, suggesting why Sher Shah termed himself a devoted son on the prayer niche of his father's tomb.

The literature dealing with Sher Shah thus presents dual images of the sultan, not totally reconcilable with each other. On one hand, there is the man who became sultan not as a result of the customary and expected good birth or high-ranking lineage, but through cunning and treachery. On the other hand, there is the picture of this ruler famed for his justice and concerned with the welfare of the ordinary man. We might credit the latter to a romanticized image of Sher Shah that developed after his death, largely by late 16th- and 17th-century authors. But Sher Shah's prolific patronage of utilitarian and religious architecture during his own life carried an important part of this image, implying that in practice, if not in theory, he was indeed suited for kingship. This patronage, we know from extant remains, is part of reality, not the myth.

Sher Shah's patronage of tombs served a similar purpose. That is, they served to elevate his lineage by posthumously glorifying his deceased ancestors and thus indicating his suitability for kingship. Further, the size and shapes of these tombs provide an explanation for their construction. The Sultan's own

11

Tomb of Sikandar Lodi, Lodi Gardens, New Delhi, circa 1517.

12

Signage for the tombs of Sher Shah Sur and Hasan Sur Shah, Sasaram, Bihar, late 20th century.

tomb at Sasaram is octagonal, a type during this period usually reserved for Afghan royalty, but it is much larger and placed in a more spectacular setting than any of its precedents. Moreover, the tank in which the tomb is situated, as well as the tomb's octagonal shape are, as we have noted, symbols of paradise. According to texts on kingship, the eternal reward of a just and pious ruler was indeed paradise. This symbolism, together with the fact that at the time of its construction it was the largest tomb in India, suggests that the patron and ruler wished to be remembered as extraordinary.

The tomb type selected for Sher Shah's grandfather is but a grander and much more carefully crafted version of the type generally reserved for high-ranking nobles of the previous Lodi dynasty. For example, square-plan tombs of high-ranking Lodi nobles are generally small and made of roughly hewn stone covered with a stucco veneer (figure 10). By contrast, the tomb of Sher Shah's grandfather, Ibrahim Sur, who was far lower in station, is substantially larger and made of finely carved masonry. Sher Shah's father Hasan Sur is buried in an octagonal tomb, a type usually reserved for royalty during this period, exemplified by the tomb of Sikandar Lodi (d. 1517) in Delhi (figure 11). The tomb of Hasan Sur is 12 metres larger in diameter and is much higher proportionally than Sikandar Lodi's tomb.

Sher Shah thus bestowed prestige upon his forebears, albeit posthumously. The trappings of good descent were essential in the case of Sher Shah, whose personal character before attaining the Delhi throne hardly warranted the status he achieved. Thus in a

sense these tombs served as visual forms of legitimation for the Sur name in much the same fashion that some earlier Islamic dynasties produced fictitious genealogies to prove their royal worthiness.

Each tomb, by mere dint of its overall appearance, served to elevate the status of the Sur name and by doing so, created a legacy suitable for a king. That the legacy created by these tombs is apparent even today may be gleaned from a sign placed before the tomb of Sher Shah's grandfather Ibrahim Sur, and another in close proximity to the tomb of his father Hasan Sur. These structures, erected by Sher Shah for his horse trader grandfather and his low-ranking father, are today identified by the Archaeological Survey of India as the tombs of Ibrahim Shah and Hasan Sur Shah (figure 12). It is as if the Survey, properly awed by the tombs and the meaning implied by them, bestowed upon Sher Shah's forebears the title Shah, which can mean either king or saint. They doubtless believed Sher Shah's message, for who but Shahs – who but kings or esteemed saints – could have such magnificent tombs?

PHOTO CREDITS

All photographs by the author, unless otherwise mentioned.

BIBLIOGRAPHY

Abbas Khan Sarwani. *The Tarikh-i-Sher Shahi*, 2 vols., trans. S.M. Imam al-Din. Dacca: University of Dacca, 1964.

Asher, Catherine B. "Legacy and Legitimacy: Sher Shah's Patronage of Imperial Mausolea", *Shari'at and Ambiguity in South Asian Islam*, ed. Katherine P. Ewing. Berkeley: University of California Press, 1988, pp. 79-97.

–. *The Patronage of Sher Shah Sur: A Study of Form and Meaning in 16th Century Indo-Islamic Architecture*. Dissertation, Minneapolis: University of Minnesota, 1984.

Nadiem, Ihsan H. *Rohtas: Formidable Fort of Sher Shah*. Lahore: Sang-e-Meel Publications, 1995.

Qanungo, Kalika Ranjan. *Sher Shah and His Time*. Bombay: Orient Longman, 1965.

1 and 2

Interior, Chhoti Masjid, Bhadresvar,
Kachchh, mid-12th century.
Photographs courtesy American
Institute of Indian Studies, Gurgaon.

ALKA PATEL

Alka Patel

From Province to Sultanate:
The Architecture of Gujarat during
the 12th through 16th Centuries

The present paper treats the architectural tradition in the region of Gujarat in western India. It is proposed here that this tradition altered as it met localized, regionally generated political, religious, and other circumstances. While the building traditions of Delhi have often been collectively emphasized as the "architectural centre" for the supposedly peripheral provinces, the evidence from Gujarat – and many other regions – favours a serious shift in this framework: it would seem that there were many architectural foci rather than a single one, urging us to modify the centre–periphery lens for viewing the multiple architectural traditions of the 12th through 16th centuries in South Asia.

Since the following architectural developments have received thorough discussion elsewhere (Patel 2004), they are summarized in brief here. The period of Gujarat's Chalukya dynasty, spanning the mid-10th through 13th centuries, coincided with the redefinition of the local temple building tradition to meet the construction demands of buildings of Islamic worship. The earliest surviving Islamic buildings of Gujarat, and possibly of India, are at Bhadresvar, Kachchh district (northwestern Gujarat). Dating to the mid-12th century, the two mosques, two tombs, and one stepwell at the site provide a critical mass of remains, and thus also furnish an overall perspective on the development of the region's Islamic architecture up to this point (Shokoohy 1988). The mosque known as the Chhoti Masjid (figure 1) demonstrates the application of temple layouts and iconographies to the mosque: the composite order of columns have square, 16-sided, and circular sections one atop the other, capped with voluted brackets. This column type is familiar from 12th-century temples, as are the auspicious motifs of the stencilled leaf, hanging garland, bead-and-reel, and the stylized pot bases. These columns uphold a trabeate structure, much like the aisles surrounding temple courtyards. The mihrab (figure 2) is an unornamented niche which was likely decorated with perishable materials when under worship (Shokoohy 1988).

The building known as the shrine of Ibrahim is likely a tomb. The interior follows the typology of the temple porch in its square-to-octagon transition, culminating in an ornate concentric ceiling. The plain mihrab is indicated on the exterior with a rounded projection (figure 3), itself graced with the mouldings which were used in temple iconography to mark the *mulaprasada* or sanctum. From the perspective of Islamic building traditions, such a configuration was clearly a translation of the domed cube into local constructional and iconographic terms. The domed cube was the archetypal funerary or commemorative structure of Islam, and was ubiquitous throughout Iran and Central Asia. Local craftspeople relied on their inherited skills to build for immigrant Muslim communities. Thus, they used the temple porch as a precedent for the making of this funerary structure, as this architectural component most closely approximated the domed cube, much more than any other component from the region's building vocabulary.

Although the buildings of Bhadresvar are parsimonious when compared with later examples, their integration of large structural components with minute iconographies in an Islamic context, and their overall accomplished presence, indicates that locally trained craftspeople had been building for Muslim communities in the region for a few generations before. This indication is bolstered by textual references to Muslim mercantile settlements in the coastal cities and other entrepots of Gujarat since at least the 9th century, and perhaps earlier (Patel 2004).

As a province of the Delhi-based Khaljis and Tughluqs during the 14th century, Gujarat remained on its localized developmental path. The typological distinctions we saw before – namely the closed temple porch interpreted as tomb, and multiplied aisles as a mosque – were combined in unprecedentedly large-scale buildings of both functions. Examples include the congregational mosque of Khambhat of 1325 (figure 4), built by the wealthy merchant Daulat Shah ibn Muhammad al-Butamari; and the addorsed tomb of another prosperous merchant, al-Kazeruni (figure 5), dating to circa 1333. The mosque of Khambhat is no longer a series of parallel aisles as we saw at Bhadresvar, but a combination of narrow aisles framing polygonal bays with concentric ceilings. The latter had been preponderant in tomb structures at Bhadresvar, and are here incorporated into the mosque typology. Al-Kazeruni's tomb also shows this amalgamation, and further has an upper storey.

3
Exterior, mihrab projection, Shrine of Ibrahim, Bhadresvar, Kachchh.
Photograph courtesy American Institute of Indian Studies, Gurgaon.

4
Interior, Congregational Mosque, Khambhat, founded 1325.
Photograph courtesy American Institute of Indian Studies, Gurgaon.

5

Tomb of al-Kazeruni.
Khambhat, circa 1333.
Photograph: Alka Patel.

6

Interior, Congregational
Mosque, Bharuch, founded
1321.
Photograph courtesy American
Institute of Indian Studies,
Gurgaon.

A notable change in the construction practices of the region during the 14th century – and one that has received much attention in scholarly and lay circles alike – was the incorporation of reused materials in these larger buildings. The Congregational Mosque of Bharuch (figure 6), dating to 1321 and also patronized by al-Butamari, is the earliest known building to recycle older architectural components. This mosque apparently established a convention followed in virtually all the 14th-century Islamic foundations of Gujarat.

Although textual sources such as court histories often assign Islamic propaganda to these instances of reuse, the reasons for the practice must have been broader. The administration of Gujarat as the province of an Islamic power, beginning in 1304 with the Khalji annexation, could have been influential on the status of buildings as state properties: now, dilapidated or even deliberately dismantled structures could be quarried by builders for the basic building blocks of later foundations.

Moreover, many of the important buildings, such as the Congregational Mosques of Bharuch and Khambhat, were commissioned by wealthy merchants rather than the Delhi-deputed provincial governors. These merchants continued in their commercial enterprises with little regard for changing political climes. After all, one could argue that it was their commercial prosperity – and not any sultan – that endowed them with power and consequence enough to patronize major social institutions such as congregational mosques. There seems to have been a delicate play and balance of power between the state and its representatives on the one hand, and on the other the economic sustenance of the region as vested in these astute merchants. In light of this play and balance, the idea of a unified agenda in religious propaganda – or anything else, for that matter – appears noticeably problematic.

Concomitant with altered administrative status and merchant patronage, we must bear in mind the sudden explosion in architectural scale during the 14th century. While the 12th-century Bhadresvar structures had been single-bay or two to three aisles on plan, these later mosques and tombs had at least three large bays, as at Bharuch, reaching up to nine bays with framing aisles at Mangrol in the congregational mosque dating to 1383. This building was

7

Interior, south bay, Congregational Mosque, Bharuch.
Photograph: Alka Patel.

8

Interior, mosque of Ahmad
Shah, Ahmadabad, circa 1411.
Photograph: Dinesh Mehta.

commissioned by one Izz al-Din ibn Aramshah, who
was also likely a wealthy merchant based in this port
city, akin to al-Butamari and al-Kazeruni at
Khambhat.

One more important consideration mitigates
against assuming Islamic propaganda to be the
exclusive reason for these instances of architectural
recycling. Studies of reuse in South Asia have not only
grouped the various instances together, but have thus
far failed to analyse the placement and integration of
the fragments in the individual buildings. A more
careful examination of the Bharuch mosque, for
example, proves to be extremely useful.

Analysis of the buildings reveals that simple,
unadorned columns and ceilings comprise the
flanking north and south bays (figure 7) of the
prayer area. By contrast, the central bay is
emphasized by proportionally heavier and more
ornate elements. The entrance into the central bay
is also highlighted by such columns, producing an
axial emphasis on the focus of prayer. This
architectural device was widespread in mosques
throughout the Islamic lands.

But the tools of axial emphasis at Bharuch were
columns recycled from earlier structures, which tended
to be more ornate than their newly carved

counterparts. Their figural imagery was often effaced
in a token fashion. Thus, while literary conventions
in Islamic court chronicles called for these older
elements to be labelled objectionable and worthy of
defilement, their physical function as emphases of the
central and most sacred part of the building suggests
that they were deployed and received with many other
meanings.

Paradoxically then, the reduction of Gujarat to a
Delhi-administered province fuelled the construction
of buildings on monumental scales, as the prosperous
merchant-magnates vied with the Khalji- and
Tughluq-deputed governors for political recognition
in the eyes of their Delhi overlords. What is more,
the seemingly sudden increase in building size was
surely a factor leading to the incorporation of older
materials, which greatly expedited construction of
such unprecedentedly large buildings.

With the establishment of the Ahmad-Shahi
sultanate in the first decade of the 15th century, the
political centre shifted back to Gujarat itself. It remains
to be seen whether there was a dialogue between the
newly established *political* centre in Gujarat and the local
architectural traditions, which over the centuries had been
adapted to the building needs of the economically
powerful Muslim communities of the region.

In 1411, the forceful and possibly patricidal Ahmad Shah (r. 1411–42) took over the sultanate of Gujarat and declared it independent of the already waning Tughluq power of Delhi. With this act he also established the dynastic capital at Ahmadabad in central Gujarat, leaving the old centre of Patan in the north to decline and gradually fade away. His indomitable personality has loomed large in the history of the dynasty, as much because of his patronage of learning as for his supposed iconoclastic zeal. Beginning with the reign of this powerful sultan and extending through that of the famous Mahmud Shah I "Begada" (r. 1458–1511), Gujarat witnessed a protracted period of architectural magnificence.

The practice of recycling materials from previously standing structures continued into the 15th century. In fact, Ahmad Shah's reputation as an iconoclast has been based largely on the buildings of his patronage which incorporated older components. Ahmadabad's first Congregational Mosque of 1411, for example, is replete with recycled materials. Equally notable is the increased scale, as the mosque consists of ten large polygonal bays in two parallel rows of five bays each.

But once again, like the Bharuch Congregational Mosque, reception of the reused components is not as unified or as transparent as scholarship has so far indicated. In all the off-centre bays of the mosque, the reused and more ornate shafts were placed above the more austere, newly carved columns. However, in the principal bay (figure 8) housing the central mihrab, the old and new are inverted, so that the reused shafts are on the bottom supporting the newly carved columns above. Furthermore, the entrance aisle of the mosque, through which the worshipper first passes upon entering the prayer hall, is emphatically delineated with ornate older shafts and ceilings.

The instance of reuse which is perhaps the most demonstrative of the ambiguous meanings older fragments carried is the Rudramahalaya/Congregational Mosque of Siddhpur, northern Gujarat (figure 9). Shortly after his accession in 1414, Ahmad Shah transformed this mid-12th-century Shaiva complex into the city's congregational mosque. The circumstances surrounding Ahmad Shah's campaign to this site in north Gujarat are unclear, though it is reasonable to assume that the sultan came to confront the recalcitrant rajas of Idar and other

9

Exterior, *qibla* wall, Rudramahalaya/Congregational Mosque, Siddhpur, circa 1140/1414.
Photograph: Alka Patel.

northern principalities still refusing to accept his overlordship.

Although the conversion of the large temple complex into Siddhpur's Jami Masjid certainly received shrift in the sultanate's chronicles as an act of religious and political domination, a closer look at the physical remains of the metamorphosis renders these interpretations less than satisfactory. While the complex's principal temple was completely dismantled, its minor shrines were left standing and uneffaced (see figure 9). In fact, these minor shrines formed both the mihrab projections on the *qibla* wall, as well as the mihrabs themselves in the prayer area. Just as we saw in the 14th century, here also is an

inherent polarity in the reception of reused components: while the act of dismantling and reincorporation can be tantamount to desecration – and is often described as such in court histories – the specific placement and function of the resulting fragments within the fabrics of later buildings seems to suggest other, even opposite, interpretations (Patel 2004a). Moreover, this polarity of meaning during the 15th century was present in mosques commissioned by the sultan himself, in contrast to the merchant patronage of mosques in the 14th century.

Architectural reuse appears to have been a leitmotif throughout the 15th- and early 16th-century buildings of the Ahmad-Shahi sultanate. Most notably, it was practised alike in structures of religious and non-religious functions, and commissioned not only by sultans but their courtiers as well. In addition to mosques, structures like stepwells also exhibited recycled elements. The Adalaj Vav (figure 13) dates to the very end of the 15th and early 16th centuries, and was commissioned by the lady consort of a local chief and ally of Sultan Mahmud Shah "Begada". It is a descending underground stepwell. Like all such foundations, it served the multiple functions of shelter from heat and rain, and also as a social gathering place.

While the walls have some smaller reused fragments tucked into corners not immediately visible (figure 10), an old sculptural relief is prominent at the pinnacle of the well shaft, occupying what seems to be pride of place. From this example along with others, it would appear that the intentional placement of reused materials – akin to the arrangements seen above in 14th- and 15th-century mosques – occurred in non-religious structures as well. Also, many of these buildings were not patronized by the reigning sultan, but by his courtiers and allies.

Sacred and non-religious structures shared more than recycled materials; they often had form and iconography also in common. With the burgeoning size of buildings throughout the 15th century, mosques came to have multiple mezzanine storeys (figures 11 and 12), the purpose of which remains unclear. But their comparability with multi-storey non-religious structures like stepwells (figures 13–15) is eminent. Such similarities suggest that mosques had also come to serve social and other functions similar to those assigned above to stepwells.

Most strikingly, iconographic details connected religious and non-religious structures in telling ways.

10

Reused relief from Adalaj Vav, Ahmadabad, 1498.

Photograph: Pramod Mistry.

11
Upper storey, Congregational
Mosque, Champaner,
circa 1506.
Photograph: Pramod Mistry.

12

Interior, upper storey,
Congregational Mosque,
Champaner.
Photograph: Pramod Mistry.

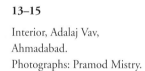

13–15
Interior, Adalaj Vav,
Ahmadabad.
Photographs: Pramod Mistry.

16

Congregational Mosque,
Ahmadabad, 1424.
Photograph: Dinodia Photo
Library/Nirmal P. Masurekar.

17

Teen Darwaza, Ahmadabad,
circa 1411–40.
Photograph: Dinodia Photo
Library/Anil A. Dave.

The similarities between the second and present Congregational Mosque of Ahmadabad (figure 16) dating to 1424, and the urban gateway known as the Teen Darwaza (figure 17) of about the same date, best demonstrate this connection. The addorsed minarets of the mosque clearly parallel the projections on the gateway. But more importantly, the mouldings defining the elevations of these architectural elements are also essentially the same. After the thin fillets at the bottom, which were variable in number and design, followed the more rigid and familiar sequence of inverted pot, torus, *cyma recta*, and roll cornice. These base mouldings were topped by the wall frieze. All of these mouldings and the wall frieze are well known not only from earlier mosques such as those of Bhadresvar, Bharuch, and Khambhat, but also from exterior temple elevations, such as the minor shrines still standing at Siddhpur (see figure 9).

From this journey through the courtyards and interiors of Gujarati buildings spanning the 12th through 16th centuries, as many questions as answers regarding the region's building practices seem to emerge. Certainly, the landscape of patronage altered, as sultans and their nobles became as prominent as the merchants had been during the 14th century, if not more. But, did this change in patronage structure effect changes in architectural practice as well?

We have seen that building materials continued to be reused from province to sultanate. Moreover, during the late 15th and early 16th centuries, recycled fragments are present in buildings of religious and non-religious functions alike, patronized both by sultans and by nobles. The selective placement of reused fragments seen during the 14th century continues in force in these later sacred and other structures as well.

The commonality in architectural form and iconography of the sultanate's religious and non-religious buildings underpins a fluidity among building types, indicating that there was a spectrum between the "sacred" and the "profane" rather than a polarity. Finally, the clear and traceable continuity from Gujarat's temple architecture to mosques, stepwells, and urban gateways of the sultanate strongly indicates the continuation of building practices firmly rooted in the region.

Thus, despite the change in the scale of the buildings, architectural practices continued on a recognizable trajectory from province to sultanate. However, changes in patronage certainly affected intention and possibly also reception. This is an essential consideration in distinguishing groups or even individual buildings, warning against subsuming all architecture into an artificial and ultimately inaccurate category such as the so-called Sultanate Period.

REFERENCES

Michell, George and Snehal Shah, eds. *Ahmadabad*. Bombay: Marg Publications, 1988.

Patel, Alka. "Building Communities in Gujarat: Architecture and Society during the Twelfth through Fourteenth Centuries". *Brill's Indological Library*, Vol. 22, ed. Johannes Bronkhorst. Leiden: E.J. Brill, 2004.

Patel, Alka. "Architectural Histories Entwined: The Rudra-mahalaya/Congregational Mosque of Siddhpur, Gujarat". *Journal of the Society of Architectural Historians*, Vol. 63, No. 2 (2004a), pp. 144–63.

Shokoohy, Mehrdad and Natalie. "Bhadresvar, the Oldest Islamic Monuments in India". *Studies in Islamic Art and Architecture*, Vol. II. Leiden: E.J. Brill, 1988.

Michael Brand

The Sultanate of Malwa

The heartland of Malwa, now part of the central Indian state of Madhya Pradesh, was a triangular shaped territory pointing northwards from its base along the Narmada river at the foot of the Vindhya range. Among the major ancient cities within Malwa were Ujjain, Vidisha (Bhilsa), and Dharanagari (Dhar). Though landlocked, Malwa was strategically located on the major overland trade route between Delhi and the south of India. It functioned as an independent Muslim sultanate from the time Dilavar Khan assumed royal status as Amid Shah Daud Ghuri in AH 804/1401–02 CE until its formal annexation by Sultan Bahadur Shah of Gujarat in 937/1531. The sultans of Malwa first ruled from Dhar, and then from a new capital 35 kilometres further to the south known as both Mandu and Shadiabad (City of Joy). Mandu, Dhar, and Nalcha formed the core of the crown lands, while the rest of Malwa was divided into four districts centred in Ujjain, Sarangpur, Bhilsa, and Hushangabad. The economy was based on the cultivation of grain and the taxation of goods passing through Malwa territory. Undoubtedly the most important primary textual source for the sultanate architecture of Malwa is the *Ma'athir-i Mahmudshahi* (The Illustrious Acts of Mahmud Shah), completed in 872/ 1468 by Ali ibn Mahmud al-Kirmani, known as Shihab Hakim.[1] Although Shihab Hakim was 89 years old when he started to compile this history of the reign of Mahmud Shah Khalji (the fourth sultan, r. 1436–69), he mentions having been given access to state documents and first-hand witnesses, and that his text was checked for accuracy by the sultan himself.[2]

The 130 years of the Malwa Sultanate were tumultuous ones marked by the large-scale realignments of power and loyalty that followed the collapse of the Delhi Sultanate at the end of the 14th century after Delhi was captured and sacked by Timur in 1398. Landlocked Malwa had to contend with a complicated array of neighbours. The other newly independent Indian sultanates – Gujarat to the west, Jaunpur to the northeast, and Bidar to the south, in the Deccan – were all rivals rather than allies. Another problem for Malwa was the Hindu state of Mewar to the west in Rajasthan, whose powerful ruler, Rana Kumbha (r. 1433–68), was in little danger of outright defeat as long as Malwa and Gujarat failed to ally themselves. In fact, for the first half of the 15th century it was Gujarat that formed the main object of Malwa aggression.

Like the other new Islamic states attempting to usurp, recreate, or share the former imperial authority of the Delhi Sultanate, Malwa also had to reckon externally with the Abbasid Caliphs in Cairo and the Timurid rulers of eastern Iran and central Asia (the latter's authority was more tangible given Timur's recent victory over Delhi). Envoys representing the Abbasid Caliph al-Mustanjid visited Mahmud Shah at his camp in the Deccan in 1466, and allegedly brought an official letter of mandate along with regalia.[3] An embassy from the court of Timur's grandson Abu Said Mirza was received in 1468 at Sarangpur, and was sent back with some exotic gifts.

1

Baz Bahadur's Palace, Mandu, 1508/09. Photograph: Dinodia Photo Library/R.A. Acharya.

Dilavar Khan was appointed governor of Malwa by the Tughluq sultan of Delhi in 1391 and one of his first official activities was the renovation of Dhar's mosques. The so-called "Bhojashala" or "Kamal Maula" Mosque was restored in 795/1392–93. With its large central courtyard surrounded by a narrow arcade on the north, east, and south sides, and a deeper sanctuary hall in front of the *qibla* wall, the ground plan of this mosque bears a basic relationship with one Tughluq mosque form but, more importantly, prefigures all those constructed in the independent Sultanate of Malwa. Very soon after his declaration of independence in 1401/02, and now ruling as Amid Shah, he embarked upon a grander programme of mosque construction throughout Malwa. The first one built was in Ujjain in 1403/04, and this was soon followed by another one further east near Lalitpur in 1404. Congregational mosques were completed in Dhar in 1404/05 and Mandu in 1405/06. The Dhar mosque (figure 2), now more commonly known as

the "Lat ki Masjid" on account of an ancient iron pillar or *lat* that still lies in front of it, adds a number of features not found at the earlier Bhojashala Mosque, including a large domed entrance chamber on the east and raised chambers at each end of the hall in front of the *qibla* wall. Both the single dome in front of the central mihrab and that over the eastern entrance are true domes rather than of trabeated construction as seen at the Bhojashala Mosque. The Mandu mosque, now more commonly known as Dilavar Khan's Mosque, is smaller than its predecessor in Dhar from the previous year, and far less ambitious. It lacks, for example, a domed space in front of the central mihrab, the two raised chambers at each end of the hall in front of the *qibla* wall, and a domed eastern entrance chamber.

From this point on, Mandu becomes the unchallenged centre of architectural activity in Malwa. The location of this fortress city is spectacular: a jagged-edged, 6-kilometre-long plateau jutting out

2

Congregational Mosque, Dhar, 1404/05, view towards northwest.
Photograph: Michael Brand.

3

Hindola Mahal, Mandu,
circa 1425–1500, view towards
northwest.
Photograph: Dinodia Photo
Library/S.D. Manchekar.

from the Vindhyas 630 metres above sea level with an almost sheer drop of 400 metres at its southern edge down to the Nimar plain, which then slopes gently southwards to the banks of the Narmada. Approaching Mandu from Delhi, 1,000 kilometres to the north, ruins of villas, serais, and tombs dot the landscape along the final 10-kilometre stretch from Dhar and Nalcha before the road rises to cross a natural causeway to the plateau. A series of fortified gateways guard the last section of switchback road leading up to the Delhi Gate. The few buildings in Mandu that rise higher than tree-level are still dwarfed by the magnitude of their setting. Large bodies of water punctuate the plateau, much of which was used for farming.

The courtly architecture of Mandu has proven difficult to study, partly because none of the buildings carry inscriptions that would help with their identification. The remains of Mandu's major palace buildings are located in the northern spur of the plateau. The northern palace zone spreads around the north and east banks of the Munj Talau (a tank presumably pre-dating the Malwa sultans since it is named after an early Hindu king of Malwa) and the

north and west banks of the smaller Kapur Talau (Camphor Tank). One of the best-preserved buildings in this complex is the Hindola Mahal ("Swinging Palace") (figure 3), with its dramatically battered walls and elephant-scaled internal ramp in its northeast corner, and with suggested dates ranging from 1425 to 1500. Another is the 110-metre-long Jahaz Mahal ("Ship Palace"), set along the narrow strip of land between the two tanks (figures 4 and 5). Probably dating from the reign of Ghiyath al-Din (r. 1469–1500), the latter was most likely one of the buildings the Mughal emperor Jahangir ordered modified by his architect Abd al-Karim Mamur Khan between 1615 and 1617, when the emperor arrived for an extended stay in Mandu.[4] More ruined structures lie to the north of the Munj Talau. Due east, on the main north–south road, lies what appears to have been a large audience hall now popularly known as "Gada Shah's Shop". Continuing south, the next group of major buildings is encountered to the east of the Sagar Talau (Ocean Tank), the largest body of water on the plateau. A large caravanserai hints at the possible commercial nature of this zone. Almost 2 kilometres further south, in an area that is still primarily rural,

4 and 5

Jahaz Mahal, Mandu,
circa 1469–1500, with later
alterations 1615–17.

Above: view towards east.
Photograph: Michael Brand.

Left: view from the top.
Photograph: Dinodia Photo
Library/N.G. Sharma.

MICHAEL BRAND

lies the so-called Baz Bahadur's Palace (figure 1), actually built by Sultan Nasir al-Din Khalji in 1508/09, with Rupmati's Pavilion set above it on a hill at the very end of the plateau with spectacular views over the Nimar plain. None of these buildings has been studied in adequate detail, and nor has the whole urban and semi-urban setting of Mandu been adequately surveyed.

Amid Shah's son and successor, Hushang Shah Ghuri (r. 1406/07–1435), was the first Malwa sultan to rule for a significant period from Mandu. Almost nothing is known about him as a patron of architecture except that he started construction of the Mandu fort during the last three years before Malwa obtained independence in 1401/02 (when he was still known as Alp Khan), and that towards the end of his reign he laid the foundations for the new Congregational Mosque. The only securely datable building from Hushang's reign is the mosque near the Sagar Talau (figure 6) completed in 1432 by Malik Mughith (d. 1462), his Khalji cousin whom he had appointed wazir. Raised on a high plinth with cells set into its eastern facade on either side of a large entrance chamber, it is a far more imposing structure than Amid Shah's Congregational Mosque in Mandu from a quarter century earlier. The ornate columns in the sanctuary in front of the *qibla* wall are re-used spolia from a Hindu temple.

The most significant achievement of Malwa architecture belongs to the patronage of Malik Mughith's son, the sultan Mahmud Shah Khalji (b. 1404; r. 1436–69). Two of the latter's sisters had married Hushang's two most powerful sons, the eldest of whom had ascended the Malwa throne after Hushang's death in 1435 as Sultan Muhammad Shah. The latter only ruled for one year before he was poisoned by forces unknown. After a struggle with nobles loyal to his late brother-in-law, Mahmud Shah ascended the throne in 1436. That Shihab Hakim often refers to Mahmud Shah as "Sahib-i Qiran", a title previously reserved for Timur who had died in 1405, suggests that the Malwa sultan held ambitions beyond reference to Delhi alone.

Mahmud's great architectural achievement was a grouping of three religious and dynastic structures: a massive Congregational Mosque, the stately tomb of Hushang Shah clad in white marble, and a unique funerary madrasa, now largely ruined, but originally featuring a second dynastic tomb and a spectacular seven-storey tower. This ambitious complex transformed Mandu from a provincial capital into a new Indian centre of royal power. Situated in the middle of the narrowest part of the Mandu plateau where barely a kilometre separates gorges sweeping out to the east and west, it is laid out in a single line more than 350 metres long. Moving from west to

6
Mosque of Malik Mughith, Mandu, 1432, east facade. Photograph: Michael Brand.

7

Congregational Mosque,
Mandu, circa 1435 and
1437/38–1454, view towards
west from Madrasa.
Photograph: Michael Brand.

8

Congregational Mosque,
Mandu, sanctuary, with mihrab
and *minbar*.
Photograph: Michael Brand.

east, one finds Hushang's Tomb, the Congregational Mosque (its *qibla* wall forms the eastern wall of the tomb enclosure but there is no direct passage between them), and then, on the other side of the main north–south road, the ruins of what is now known popularly as the "Ashrafi Mahal" but is described by Shihab Hakim as the Madrasa of the Heavenly Vault (*madrasa-i bam-i bihisht*). Along with the open space between the mosque and the madrasa, they form a sequence of four square units of approximately the same dimensions. Shihab Hakim also mentions a garden behind the madrasa.[5] A pronounced ridge running from the centre of its rear facade could very well reflect the course of a paved water canal in this garden that would add a fifth similarly sized unit to the group.

Construction of the Congregational Mosque (figure 7) was commenced by Hushang Shah shortly before his death in 1435, and recommenced by Mahmud Shah in 1437/38, just after he ascended the throne of Malwa in 1436. According to Shihab Hakim:

"At this time, he [Mahmud Shah] issued ... a royal mandate ... that the Congregational Mosque, which His Late Majesty Hushang Shah ... had ordered and whose foundations he had started to excavate before the Rampol Gate, should be put in order in line with his [Hushang's] will and should be completed with a great effort .... In a short time, 230 domes resting on 380 [f. 99a] pillars, each one of which was a support of the faith and a pillar of Islam, were erected in hewn stone."[6]

An inscription above the main entrance gives the date of completion as 1454.

Faced in blocks of pink limestone, the mosque sits on a plinth almost five metres above ground level with a large domed entrance pavilion projecting east

9

Tomb of Hushang Shah, Mandu, circa 1437/38–1450. Photograph: Dinodia Photo Library/Anil A. Dave.

towards the main road. The unadorned, three-metre high square columns form a grid-pattern interrupted only by a large central courtyard and three square spaces in front of the *qibla* wall, over which domes rise more than 20 metres above floor level. The central domed space (figure 8) is set in front of the main mihrab (with polished black basalt surfaces) while the other two are set at the north and south ends of the sanctuary over chambers raised 4 metres above the main floor level. A miniature dome is set above each of the 4-metre-square modules created by the intersecting rows of columns.

Hushang's Tomb (figure 9) was built simultaneously with the mosque. It is set on a lower plinth, barely 2 metres high, in a quadrangle entered at the north from a road leading from the main palace zone. The tomb measures 21.5 metres square with a single dome rising the same distance above floor level. Entirely clad in white marble, it is remarkably pure in its form and, like the mosque, austere in its lack of ornamentation or any epigraphic programme. Three pierced marble windows are set into the north wall and two more flank the entrance door on the south. A white marble sarcophagus set in the centre of the interior is presumably that of

Hushang Shah, although it lacks any identifying inscription.

All that we know physically of the madrasa (figure 10) is that which was revealed by excavations in the early 20th century from a mound of debris 45 metres square and 10 metres high. But thanks to Shihab Hakim's long description of its glories, it still emerges as the most extraordinary individual achievement of sultanate architecture in Malwa:

"In 845 [1441/42], the highest command . . . was issued for the construction of the heaven-reaching *madrasa* [religious college], which has come to be known as the Madrasa of the Heavenly Vault [*madrasa-i bam-i bihisht*], and the building of the foundation of the minaret [*manara*] which has become famous as the Sign of Islam [*alam-i islam*]."[7]

It had still not been completed when Shihab Hakim was writing between 1466–68, and was probably only brought to conclusion during the reign of Sultan Ghiyath al-Din (1469–1500).

Describing the lower level of the structure, which rises 8 metres above ground level, Shihab Hakim notes that "on the left and right they have built a *khanqah* [hospice] and a *madrasa* in which high-ranking scholars and virtuous learned people are present each

10

Madrasa of the Heavenly Vault, Mandu, 1441/42–circa 1480, view towards east.
Photograph: Michael Brand.

day".[8] The core of the plinth does indeed appear to have been surrounded on all four sides by cells, although now only 19 of them survive on the western side. No larger communal spaces have been found on this level.

The second tomb described by Shihab Hakim sits directly above the solid core of the plinth. It measures about 27 metres square, but almost all the superstructure collapsed at some point in the 19th century. What remains of the walls are faced on both sides with white marble. On either side of windows in the north wall, there are the remains of vertical epigraphic bands of Quranic text carved into white marble blocks in a very fine Thuluth script with some yellow stone inlay (figure 11). All surviving sections of the inscription fall within verses 40 and 56 of *Sura* 36, which is characterized by warnings to the non-believers and promises of paradise to the faithful on the Day of Judgement. Shihab Hakim describes further ornamental details (some of which can be corroborated by the excavation report) that would have made this structure unique in India at the time:

11
Madrasa of the Heavenly Vault, Mandu, north interior wall of Khalji tomb.
Photograph: Michael Brand.

"They decorated its walls in all directions with coloured stones such as red cornelian, green, striped, and dark blue jasper, yellow 'Stone of Mary' [*sang-i maryam*; perhaps a variety of agate], white alabaster, black marble, and so forth in the manner that inlay workers [*khatambandan*] produce ivory and ebony decoration.... Persian workers [*amala-i fars*] ... decorated the sides of the lofty dome with tile work [*kashikari*] inscriptions in *thuluth* and *muhaqqaq* scripts of ... extreme fineness and straightness.... They strove to accomplish the joining of the knot-work [*taqid-i girabandi*] in such a manner that the engineer could not fathom the depths of its multiplicity of forms.... [I]t has been for some twenty-odd years that artists [*hunarmandan*] of dexterous hand and artisans [*pishavaran*] endowed with wisdom have dedicated themselves with elegant endeavour to the decoration [*arayish*] of the building and making it form. Yet it has still not been completed."[9]

The Portuguese Jesuit Father Anthony Monserrate saw the Madrasa intact in 1580, on his way from Goa to the court of the Mughal emperor Akbar in Fatehpur Sikri, as did Akbar's son and successor, Jahangir, during his extended stay in Mandu from 1617. It is possible to extrapolate from Monserrate's description that the dome over the tomb would have risen about 27 metres above floor level, higher than those of both the mosque and Hushang's Tomb. Jahangir wrote that the building contained the graves of Sultan Ghiyath al-Din (d. 1500) and his son, Sultan Nasir al-Din (r. 1500–10) but, because Monserrate mentioned three royal graves (with gilded thrones at their bases) and that of a "tutor", it can be assumed that this funerary madrasa was originally constructed by Mahmud Shah to contain his own tomb and that of his father, the wazir Malik Mughith, before it was also used by his two successors.

Bases of circular structures survive on all four corners of the plinth (see figure 10). The one on the northwest corner measures 48 metres in circumference and is presumably the base of the seven-storey tower Shihab Hakim describes as the "Sign of Islam". Jahangir says it had 171 steps and that each of its seven floors had four chambers with four windows apiece. Based on that number of steps, it must have stood approximately 45 metres high (in comparison, the early 13th-century Qutb Minar in Delhi has a base with a circumference of 45 metres and, with the later addition of one small extra level, still stands 72.5 metres high). The symbolic significance of the Mandu

tower is heightened by the fact that it is attached to the funerary madrasa rather than to the congregational mosque as a minaret.

Commenced within a five-year period between 1437 and 1442, the strong formal and conceptual relationship of these three buildings requires that they should be seen as a single complex rather than individual monuments. As such, it is unique within the history of sultanate architecture in India. Incorporating powerful architectural symbols as well as acting as a treasury for important dynastic regalia, the complex can be interpreted as both a major legitimization of Khalji power in Malwa and an attempt to incorporate the mark of this new power within the evolving political and religious geography of north India. It also brings into focus the relationship between Malwa sultanate architecture and that of Delhi and beyond.

First of all, it is clear that architects in sultanate Mandu, unlike those in Gujarat, were not working in a regional style, or in one that consciously continued previous traditions from the time of earlier Hindu rulers of the region. By the middle of the 15th century, these architects were working within a flexible system that was not confined by the borders of Malwa. At this stage in northern India there was at least some communality of basic building forms and decorative motifs, such as the merlon bands that are found not only in buildings constructed by Mahmud Shah in Mandu but also in those constructed for the Mewar ruler Rana Kumbha in the 1440s and 1450s, including Hindu and Jain temples in Kumbhalgarh and Ranakpur.

Looking north to Delhi, it must be remembered that the most important monuments of the Tughluq dynasty (1320–1413) date from 50 to 100 years earlier than Mahmud Shah's grand complex in Mandu. The fortress-like tomb of the Tughluq sultan Ghiyath al-Din (r. 1320–25) is similar in scale to that of Hushang Shah in Mandu but is quite different in form, especially in its use of sloping walls. The stucco-covered tomb of Firuz Shah (r. 1351–88) is smaller than both of the above tombs. The congregational mosque built by Muhammad Tughluq (r. 1325–51) at Jahanpanah in about 1343 (the so-called "Begumpuri" Mosque) establishes a basic sultanate type with its open courtyard, but the *iwan*s in the centre of each interior facade were never replicated in Malwa. The "Khirki" Mosque, from about a decade later at Jahanpanah, features corner bastions, cells in the plinth and groups of square monolithic columns, but its cross-axial floor plan is not found in any of the Malwa Sultanate's mosques. What might have been the most inspiring to Mahmud Shah was Firuz Shah's juxtaposition of the unique "Lat Pyramid", crowned by a massive Ashokan *lat* or column, directly opposite a circa 1354 mosque at Firuzabad. The "Sign of Islam" tower would have been built with a clear memory of the Qutb Minar in Delhi, but that was completed over a century before the beginning of Tughluq rule in India.

The most intriguing link of all is that suggested by Shihab Hakim's comment that "dextrous artisans and intelligent, tasteful artists, each one of whom was the chief of a clime and unique in the lands of the empire and was from the kingdoms of Khorasan and the cities of Hindustan, had gathered by the foot of the throne" for the construction of Mahmud Shah's Madrasa. The reference to Khorasan, and by inference the glories of the Timurid capital, Herat, do not appear to be entirely rhetorical. If nothing else, his description of the epigraphic decoration on the dome of Mahmud Shah's Madrasa certainly *sounds* more "Khorasani" than "Indian". Such decoration, in a variety of media, is typical of Timurid architecture that is also closer in date to Mahmud's works than the Tughluq structures in Delhi. The sheer monumentality of Mahmud Shah's Madrasa might also be seen as a contribution by these "Khorasani" architects and engineers.

The sultanate architecture of Malwa had an influence on Indian architecture even beyond the period of Mughal rule when, during the British colonial era, inspiration was being sought for the planning of New Delhi, the last great imperial capital constructed in India. In 1913, the Viceroy Lord Hardinge insisted that the architects chosen to design the new capital, Herbert Baker and Edwin Lutyens, should visit Mandu as part of their search for an appropriately "Eastern" imperial style.[10] Almost a century later, it is hoped these great examples of Indian sultanate architecture and their equally magnificent setting will inspire a new generation of a survey and scholarship as well as greater appreciation for this important phase of Indian culture.

NOTES

1.   This history has yet to be either critically edited or translated into English. For this study I have used the manuscript belonging to the Bodleian Library at Oxford University (MS. Elliot 237). Although the first few pages and the colophon of the Bodleian manuscript are missing, the bold Nashki script in which the bulk of the text is written certainly suggests that it was copied prior to the Mughal period, presumably somewhere in Malwa. For this reason it can be tentatively dated to the period between the completion of the text in 1468 and the fall of Malwa in 1531. The text was partially referenced by Upendra Nath Day in his book *Medieval Malwa: A Political and Cultural History 1401–1562* (Delhi: Munshiram Manoharlal, 1965), the major secondary source on the history of the Malwa sultanate.

2.   *Ma'athir-i Mahmudshahi*, ff. 10a–10b.

3.   *Ma'athir-i Mahmudshahi*, ff. 261b–264a.

4.   *The Jahangirnama: Memoirs of Jahangir, Emperor of India*, tr., ed., and annotated by Wheeler M. Thackston (Washington, DC: Freer Gallery of Art, 1999), pp. 169 and 213–15.

5.   *Ma'athir-i Mahmudshahi*, f. 110a.

6.   *Ma'athir-i Mahmudshahi*, ff. 98b–99a.

7.   *Ma'athir-i Mahmudshahi*, f. 108b.

8.   *Ma'athir-i Mahmudshahi*, f. 110a.

9.   *Ma'athir-i Mahmudshahi*, ff. 109a–b.

10.   Thomas R. Metcalf, "Architecture and Empire: Sir Herbert Baker and the Building of New Delhi", in *Delhi Through the Ages: Essays in Urban History, Culture and Society*, ed. R.E. Frykenberg (Delhi: Oxford University Press, 1986), p. 395.

1

Dakhil Darwaza, Gaur, 15th–16th century.
Photograph: Shiharan Nandy, courtesy of the
State Archaeological Museum, Kolkata.

Pika Ghosh

Problems of Reconstructing Bengali Architecture of the 14th–16th Centuries

The Ghurid conquest of parts of modern West Bengal was undertaken by the military commander Muhammad Bakhtiyar Khalji in 1198. He established his capital at Lakhnauti, an important city in the frontier zone between Bihar and Bengal, which had also been the capital of the Pala (730–1197/98) and Sena (12th century) dynasties. Displacing these powerful rulers of the past and substituting Ghurid control in their stead initiated the period of sultanate rule in the region. Control of Bengal by a Delhi-based power continued for nearly 140 years through the early 14th century, with the Mamluk sultans, the short-lived Khaljis, and the Tughluqs (for a brief period) successively holding the area as a province through their governors. By the 1330s, regional power had been dispersed throughout several centres, including Satgaon in southwestern Bengal and Sonargaon near modern-day Dhaka (Bangladesh). The feat of integrating these centrifugal pockets was accomplished by Ilyas Shah (r. 1339–58), who thus initiated the Ilyas-Shahi sultanate of Bengal. Similar to the dynastic feuds and upheavals in Delhi, Bengal also underwent its share of warring dynastic factions and changes of ruler until the region's annexation into the Mughal empire in 1576.

The ethnically and culturally heterogeneous rulers and court elite undertook monumental architectural projects spanning the 13th through 16th centuries. The patron groups included Turkic, Iranian, Afghan, and Ethiopian (Habshi) migrants moving east in search of economic and political opportunities, and also native Bengali dynasties such as the family of Raja Ganesh (r. 1414–18; and 1418–33). Contemporary Chinese and Portuguese travellers visiting the region attest to the grandeur of the region's courts and the highly elaborate building projects. João de Barros (1496–1570) of the Portuguese mission, for example, suggests that the Bengal sultans served as the model against which their peers measured themselves:

"Sultan Badur [Babur, 1526–30], being himself one of the richest Kings in that Orient, and very arrogant, used to say that he was one, and the King of Narsinga [Vijayanagara] two and the King of Bengal was three, meaning to say that the King of Bengal had alone, as much as he, and the King of Bisnaga [Vijayanagara] had together."[1]

This diplomat's account indicates that a very powerful state had been established in the region under the Husain-Shahi sultans. It was based on prosperous trade in agricultural commodities, silk, and cotton. The surplus from this flourishing maritime trade was invested in architecture that awed the visiting foreign dignitaries no less:

"We arrived at the second gate and we were searched as at the first, and we passed by this and by others, as many as nine and we were searched each one, and arriving the last gate, we saw a great courtyard the length of a great track, and half hollow, and so wide, or wider than [it was] long on which twelve men were playing *choqua*-polo on horseback, and at the end of the said courtyard a great dais was set upon thick props of sandalwood, and those above, upon which the roof rested, were not as thick, all carved with *maçanarya*-joinery and [with] many gilded branches and small birds, and the ceiling above in the same manner, and [with] a moon and a sun, with [a] very great number of stars, and all gilded. We arrived to where the King was seated on a very great catere-divan, likewise gilded, with [a] very large store of great and small pillows, all embroidered, and with many precious stones and seed-pearls on them…."[2]

This architecture must therefore be seen as a product of the wealthy and highly cosmopolitan order created during the reigns of these dynasties.

Numerous scholars have surveyed and classified the extant monuments.[3] The more interpretive studies read the succession of monuments as a narrative of increasing localization, with foreign dynasties rooting themselves politically and culturally in local soil, thus following trends established in the rest of the Islamic world. Most recently, Perween Hasan has pointed to the use of local elements such as the *chala*, the curved roof associated with the sag of the thatch piled on hut roofs, and the thatch-roofed hut as a model for the single-domed mosque (figures 4, 6, 7, and 13).[4] The huge, pillared courtyard mosque, preferred in Iran and northern India, was attempted only once in Bengal by Sultan Sikandar Shah (r. 1358–90) of the Ilyas-Shahi dynasty at the Adina Masjid (1374–75) in Hazrat Pandua (figures 2 and 3). The smaller, more contained monuments were much more prolifically patronized and seemed to share affinities with the hut architecture of the region. The overwhelming preference for the latter type of building has been explained as a response to the local geographic and climatic elements that deter travel over great distances

2 and 3

Adina Masjid, interior, central mihrabs with *minbar*, Hazrat Pandua, 1374–75. Photographs: (above) Pika Ghosh, (below) Shiharan Nandy, courtesy of the State Archaeological Museum, Kolkata.

in the face of floods and torrential rain. Likewise, the creative reuse of pre-existing carved stone slabs for mihrabs and *minbar*s, often fragments from Pala-period Buddhist or Hindu temples, is attributed to the foreign patrons' positive predisposition and receptiveness toward local material (figures 8–11).[5] The scholars espousing this interpretation consider the architectural choices of the patrons as political manoeuvres for control, alleviating the foreignness of the ruling courts, and offering a cultural environment that was fertile for creativity in the construction of mosques and mausolea.

Much of the scholarly literature on Bengal has, however, equated "Islamic" with "sultanate". This unexamined equation is borne out by the studies' focus on mosques, for example, rather than the many unidentified buildings. An alternative approach to the 13th through 16th centuries of Bengal's architectural history would take into account what does not survive either due to accident or design, such as palaces and non-elite residences. The absence of palatial structures at the various sultanates' capitals of Lakhnauti, Pandua, and Gaur do not automatically lead one to

conclude that such buildings never existed. Rather, their absence suggests that, instead of mosques, tombs, and shrines, the buildings associated explicitly with political authority were likely to have been the primary targets of groups competing for power. The classification of architecture by dynasties, and indeed by the very term "sultanate", both inevitably imply a "top down" approach which ignores subaltern histories. The inadequacy of this approach is also apparent when we consider that constructions in less expensive and less permanent materials by a host of lower classes have also been erased from the historical record.

It is further necessary to consider what is typically excluded from the traditional narratives that focused on the burst of architectural innovations clustered in the capital cities, and to re-examine what survives across the region from the 13th century to the Mughal conquest of 1576. For example, an inscription found in the village of Siwan records the construction of a Sufi *khanqah* as early as the 13th century.[6] The presence of a stable Muslim zamindari in Birbhum was probably responsible for the constructions in this

4

Chota Sona Masjid, Gaur, 1493–1519. Note the central four-eaved hut form of the roof. Photograph: Pika Ghosh.

region. Ambika-Kalna, in Burdwan district, flaunts the ruins of five substantial structures. The city of Bardhaman was famous for the dargah of Pir Bahram Saqqa, a typical monument of the mid-16th century (1562). The monuments at Tribeni and the ruins of a fort and the dargah of Shah Ismail Ghazi at Garh-Mandaran attest to sultanate architecture in southwestern Bengal from the end of the 13th century. Together they suggest the reach of the period style to the borders of Orissa.

The evidence of shared architectural elements and vegetal motifs suggests that missing secular monuments would have been significant for defining style in this period, which can no longer be associated

7

Domestic hut, Birbhum district.
Photograph: Shiharan Nandy,
courtesy of the State
Archaeological Museum,
Kolkata.

8

Adina Masjid, detail of door
lintel. Photograph: Shiharan
Nandy, courtesy of the
State Archaeological Museum,
Kolkata.

exclusively with "Islamic" architecture. The presence of dated Hindu temples from the period also attests to the need to redefine "sultanate" style in broader terms.

The description of an imposing palace and luxuriant court within the ramparts of the citadel cited above suggests the presence of monumental palatial architecture, which was surely accompanied by elite residences to support the courtly infrastructure. None has survived, however, thereby limiting our corpus to mosques, mausolea, and a few city gates and unidentified buildings that may have been madrasas, resthouses, and warehouses (figures 1 and 13). What remain standing are therefore survivors from a much larger body of buildings that have perished for a variety of reasons, including the merciless monsoons and the dense vegetation they nurture. Banyan trees erupting through brick and mud ruins at Kulut, at the border between Birbhum and Bardhaman, for example, testify to the presence of a significant structure, perhaps a resthouse, adorned with exquisite vegetal terracotta panels in the distinctive style of the early 16th century (figure 12). When compared with the

9–11

Bari Dargah (tomb of Shah Jalal
d. 1337), Hazrat Pandua, and
details of pillars. Photographs:
Shiharan Nandy, courtesy of the
State Archaeological Museum,
Kolkata.

beautiful, better-preserved mosques of Gaur and
Hazrat Pandua (see figures 2 and 3), ruins such as
those of Kulut indicate that there were probably many
more innovations and variations in the architecture
of this period which are no longer discernible.

Likewise, 300 years have left their mark on the
survivors. Most have been altered, modified by
generations of users who made the space their own,
particularly at sacred sites such as the dargahs at the
capital cities of Hazrat Pandua and Gaur (figures 9–
11). These monuments disclose dramatic shifts in
appearance created by closing entrances, extending
porches, and similar modifications. In other cases, the
incorporation of a niche in the west wall to serve as a
mihrab suggests that buildings were reoriented and
put to new uses over time. Moreover, stripping the
heavy white lime plaster, which previously protected
the terracotta surfaces, has significantly changed their
appearance. Coloured and glazed ceramic tiles on the
late 15th-century Lattan Masjid and Gumti Darwaza
at Gaur suggest that colour was a significant
component of the period aesthetic. Other buildings
that continue to be in private hands are repainted
regularly, flaunting vivid colours which highlight the
terracotta sculptural ornament. They remind us of the
aesthetic shifts that occur over 500 years, and point
to the divergent interests of devotional communities
to maintain a ritually potent building, and those of
archaeological preservation driven by a modernist
preference for terracotta rather than bright paint.
Although monuments standing before us offer a
tangible experience of the past, they yet remain

12

Ruined structure at Kulut, early 16th century.
Photograph: Pika Ghosh.

13

Chika Masjid, Gaur, late 15th–early 16th century.
Photograph: Shiharan Nandy, courtesy of the
State Archaeological Museum, Kolkata.

tantalizing, for there is no unmediated view into the time and place from which they came.

As noted, the majority of surviving architectural evidence in Bengal from the 13th through 16th centuries consists mostly of mosques, tombs, and shrines. This considerably skews our understanding of the architecture of the period. Other than the crumbling boundary walls with imposing gates at Gaur, little survives by way of urban civic structures. Indeed, what little survives at Gaur indicates stylistic continuity across secular and sacred structures. The heavy buttresses distinguishing Gaur's massive gateways are also used for its mosques (figures 1, 5, 13, and 14). Terracotta ornamental motifs, such as flowers encased in pointed arches, extend in horizontal bands across the bastions of both gateways and mosque surfaces. Nevertheless, the overwhelming presence of explicitly religious monuments in the historical record has rendered the terms "Islamic" and "sultanate" virtually synonymous, despite the richness and variety of religious beliefs and practices we find from the period.

The mosques and tombs associated with the late-15th to mid-16th centuries share elements such as shallow domes, low facades, brick and terracotta decoration, and the curved cornices of the local thatch-roofed huts (figures 4–7, 13, and 14). In addition, they share with the huts their fundamental organizational framework, clustered around an interior courtyard and bounded by a low mud-brick wall. In the traditional domestic compound, the hut closest to the entrance, often no more than a covered porch, is usually where visitors are received, while inner ones are for sleeping, cooking, grain storage, cow pens, and domestic shrines. Such organization allows large joint families to reside and perform multiple functions within a single enclosure. This division of spaces for various activities within the domestic complex parallels the walled mosque enclosures with ablution areas, burial grounds, shrines for local holy men, and perhaps a hall for ceremonial meals, aside from the main prayer chamber. Although many mosque complexes retain the gates and

enclosure walls, most of these additional structures have fallen away. Bagha and Shura are rare examples with multiple surviving structures (see figure 14). These commonalities with modern homesteads also suggest that elite residential complexes from the period likely shared such features with sacred architecture.

Colonial scholars of the 19th century, with their heavy emphasis upon religion as the basis for understanding Bengal's architecture, also ignored the Hindu temples built during this period. Although not abundant, temples do remain from this period, from as far west as Purulia district to the Sundarbans in the south, and suggest a variety of experiments with available architectural styles and ornament. Temple Nos. 1 and 2 at Barakar, Bardhaman district (1461), suggest that the Nagara style of curvilinear towered temples, which dominated north India, continued to be built (figure 15). Others such as the Krishna temple at Baidyapur, Bardhaman district (1598), modified the curvilinear profile of the tower to terminate in the four-eaved hut roofs (*charchala*). This profile was

14

Jami Masjid, Bagha, 1523.
Photograph: Pika Ghosh.

also used in 15th- and 16th-century mosques, such as the Chota Sona Masjid (1493–1519) at Gaur (see figure 4).

In ornamentation as well, the 16th-century temples at Baidyapur, the Bhairavi temple at Bindol, West Dinajpur district, the Mathurapur Deul at Madhukeli, Faridpur district, and the Radha Damodar Temple at Ghutgeriya, Bankura district (figure 16), share stylistic elements with the mosques and shrines of the 16th century. These include the Qadam Rasul (1530), the Dakhil Darwaza (see figure 1), Dhunichak Masjid, the Jami Masjid at Bagha (1523), the mosques at Goaldi (1519), and Kushumba (1558). At Baidyapur and Ghutgeriya, the entrance to the Nagara

temple takes the form of a cusped, pointed arch supported on engaged pilasters and flaunting high-relief lotus blossoms on the arch spandrels. This organization is similar to what we find on Gaur's gates, shrines, and mosques (see figure 16).[7] Like Baidyapur, the Mathurapur Deul also inserts these decorative features onto the Nagara body of the temple. The Nagara surface is sheathed with horizontal bands of delicate organic and geometric terracotta decoration, similar in treatment to those at Bagha, for instance.[8] The ruined temple at Bindol is adorned with both the running vegetal motifs and panels akin to those at Kulut. These monuments testify to a style shared by mosques and temples, challenging the easy conflation of a "sultanate" style with Islam in Bengal.

Early British studies of Bengal architecture, however, defined extant monuments as either Hindu or Islamic, treating them as disparate traditions, the former indigenous and the latter imposed. A political climate that could allow for interaction among the region's different religious and artistic communities could not be imagined within the available colonial and post-colonial conceptual frameworks. Thus, Bengal's cultural history was characterized according to race and religion, two categories which were typically conflated in defining group identities.

With the production of colonial knowledge during the 19th century, such identification of people and monuments had come to dominate. British administrators invoked these categories in part to justify and maintain colonial institutions. Their historians, ethnographers, site surveyors, and cartographers propagated them in the documentation and description they compiled toward consolidating British territorial acquisitions.[9] These colonial perceptions of religion did not acknowledge the fluidity of identity that we are now beginning to recognize.[10]

Writing in the mid-20th century, the architectural historian Percy Brown remained reluctant to discard these categories, despite the failure of the visual evidence to conform: "[In] no part of India are the two great cultural movements, the Hindu and the Muhammedan and the manner in which the one superseded the other more vividly illustrated than in some of the ancient remains of Bengal…."[11] He continued to group monuments by ruling dynasties, conflated with religious affiliations, treating Bengal prior to the 13th century as Hindu and ignoring the rich and complex interaction between the patronage

and production of Hindu and Buddhist temples. He then characterized the post-13th-century history of Bengal as Islamic, which although true of the rulers, cannot of course be said of the population in its entirety, which included substantial Hindu communities as well as Muslim.

Nor do the labels "Hindu" and "Muslim" satisfactorily distinguish the newly converted Muslim populace from the Hindu Bengalis. Brown's brief discussion of Bengal architecture is spread thinly through two volumes. The first, *The Islamic Period*, contains the discussion of the mosques, while his discussion of temples which precede as well as succeed these mosques is located in a chapter titled "The Brahmanical Buildings of Bengal (8th to 17th centuries)". Brown ignored chronology and instead conflated religious practices, the religious orientation

of monuments, building techniques, and art historical styles under the rubric of religion. By giving primacy to religion, he remained unable to examine the complex relationships between structures, patrons, artisans, and the particular historical circumstances informing the formal choices for monumental construction.

Yet, literary works from the period suggest continuities in artistic traditions despite the divergent religious orientations of patrons. In Mukundaram's *Kavikankan Chandi* of the late 16th-century, for example, the construction of the mythical city of Gujarat, inspired by the Goddess Chandi, included Muslim workers.[12]

A review of the discourses that gathered around Bengal's 13th- through 16th-century architecture thus uncovers the ideologies circulated in colonial literature

16

Doorway, Radha Damodar Temple, Ghutgeriya, late 16th century. Photograph: Pika Ghosh.

and institutional practices. Here, I have probed one basic assumption underlying the studies of this material, the easy equation of "sultanate" with "Islamic", pointing to its incongruence with the architectural record. The range of available materials provides instead a glimpse of a wealthy, cosmopolitan, and culturally rich and diverse world. Not only the sultans, but also local Hindu and Muslim landholders patronized a variety of buildings, likely deploying their resources to compete for power and prestige.

NOTES

1. João de Barros, *Da Asia*, Decada IV Livro IX Capitulo I, cited in Ronald Bishop Smith, *The First Age of the Portuguese Embassies and Peregrinations to the Ancient Kingdoms of Cambay and Bengal (1500–1521)* (Bethesda, MD: Decatur Press, 1969), p. 133.

2. Anonymous, *Lembrança dalgumas coussas que se passaram quando Amtonio de Bryto e Dyogo Pereyra foram a Bemgalla asy em Bengala como em Tanaçaiym e em Pegu onde tambem fomo*, São Vicente: Vol. 11, pp. 47–88, cited in Bishop Smith, *The First Age*, p. 91.

3. Perween Hasan, "Sultanate Mosque-Types in Bangladesh: Origins and Development", Ph.D. dissertation, Harvard University, 1984; Ahmad Hasan Dani*, Muslim Architecture of Bengal* (Dacca: Asiatic Society of Pakistan, 1961); Catherine B. Asher, "Inventory of Key Monuments" in George Michell, ed., *The Islamic Heritage of Bengal* (Paris: UNESCO, 1984); Abid Ali Khan, *Memoirs of Gaur and Pandua*, edited and revised by H.E. Stapleton (Calcutta: Bengal Secretariat Book Depot, 1931); Henry Creighton, *The Ruins of Gaur* (London: Black, Parbury and Allen, 1817).

4. Perween Hasan, "Sultanate Mosques and Continuity in Bengal Architecture", *Muqarnas* 6 (1989), pp. 68–73; "The Footprint of the Prophet", *Muqarnas* 10 (1993), pp. 335–47; and "Temple Niches and Mihrabs in Bengal", in Anna Libera Dallapicolla and Stephanie Lallemant, eds., *Islam and Indian Regions* (Stuttgart: Franz Steiner Verlag, 1993), pp. 86–94.

5. Ralph Pinder-Wilson, "Stone Sculptures of Gaur", in John Guy, ed., *Indian Art Connoisseurship: Essays in Honor of Douglas Barrett* (Delhi: Indira Gandhi National Centre for the Arts and Mapin Publishing Pvt. Ltd., 1996), pp. 251–61; Naseem Ahmed Banerji, "The Architecture and Architectural Decoration of the Adina Mosque, Pandua, West Bengal, India: The Problem of the Conjoined Buddhist, Hindu, and Islamic Motifs in the Mihrab Niches," Ph.D. dissertation, University of Iowa, 1993.

6. This stone tablet, dated July 29, 1221, is probably the earliest Muslim inscription in Bengal. Z.A. Desai, "An Early Thirteenth-Century Inscription from West Bengal," *Epigraphia Indica, Arabic and Persian Supplement* (1975), pp. 6–12.

7. See Pika Ghosh, *Temple to Love: Architecture and Devotion in Seventeenth-Century Bengal* (Bloomington IN: Indiana University Press and American Institute of Indian Studies), pp. 112–13.

8. In addition, figural forms and narrative sequences are introduced in these temples. See Ghosh, p. 113.

9. Tapati Guha-Thakurta, *The Making of a New Indian Art* (Cambridge: Cambridge University Press, 1992); Partha Mitter, *Much Maligned Monsters: A History of European Reactions to Indian Art* (1977; reprint, Chicago: University of Chicago Press, 1992); Catherine B. Asher and Thomas R. Metcalf, eds., *Perceptions of South Asia's Visual Past* (New Delhi and Madras: American Institute of Indian Studies and Swadharma Swarajya Sangha, 1994).

10. Richard M. Eaton, *The Rise of Islam and the Bengal Frontier 1204–1760* (Berkeley: University of California Press, 1995).

11. Percy Brown, *Indian Architecture*, vol. 1: *The Buddhist and Hindu Period* (1942; reprint, Bombay: D.B. Taraporevala Sons and Co. Pvt. Ltd., 1965), p. 149.

12. Mukundaram Chakrabarty, *Kavikankan Chandi*, eds. Srikumar Bandyopadhyay and Visvapati Chaudhuri (Calcutta: Calcutta University, 1974), pp. 343–61.

Phillip B. Wagoner

The Charminar as *Chaubara*: Cosmological Symbolism in the Urban Architecture of the Deccan

The Deccan plateau of southern India became part of the territory of the Delhi Sultanate only in the Khalji and Tughluq periods. In the second and third decades of the 14th century, vast tracts of this Marathi, Kannada, and Telugu speaking region were incorporated as provinces under Delhi's rule, and old Deccani cities like Deogiri and Warangal were renamed and rebuilt as outposts of the sultanate. Mosques, palatial buildings, and other public monuments sprang up under direct sultanate patronage, bringing about the rapid dissemination of the metropolitan style of Khalji and Tughluq Delhi. Within less than another two decades, however, the ruling elite of the Deccani provinces had proclaimed their independence from Delhi, and founded their own Bahmani Sultanate which dominated the northern part of the Deccan from 1347 until its effective demise around 1500. During the Bahmani period, Deccani architecture gradually moved away from its Khalji and Tughluq roots, in favour of a more distinctive local style that owed as much to Timurid Persian and local, pre-Sultanate forms and ideas as it did to the models of Delhi. By the early 16th century, the Bahmani Sultanate had disintegrated, giving way to five successor states, of which three – the Adil Shahi Sultanate of Bijapur, the Nizam Shahi Sultanate of Ahmadnagar, and the Qutb Shahi Sultanate of Golconda-Hyderabad – rose to pre-eminence in both the political and the architectural spheres. The architectural output of these three sultanates was profuse as well as innovative, and remained vital until each state was finally incorporated into the expanding Mughal empire during the course of the 17th century. The concept of "Sultanate Architecture" in the Deccan is thus a complex and multifaceted one, embracing three very distinct traditions: first, the architecture of the Deccan province of the Delhi Sultanate under the Khaljis and Tughluqs; second, the architecture of the independent Deccani Sultanate of the Bahmanis; and third, the architectural products of the three main Bahmani successor states centred on Bijapur, Ahmadnagar, and Golconda-Hyderabad.[1]

1

The Charminar at Hyderabad, view from the north.

2

The fountain at the centre of the
Charminar's ground level.

3

Charminar, mosque on upper
storey, view of prayer hall.
Photograph: ACSAA Slide
#2386 © AAAUM.

Rather than attempting a comprehensive survey of the totality of Deccani Sultanate architecture, this essay provides an in-depth examination of just one late-16th-century monument from the Qutb Shahi Sultanate. This monument is the Charminar, constructed in 1591 under the patronage of Sultan Muhammad Quli Qutb Shah in the new capital city of Hyderabad (figure 1). Although it may be the best-known monument from Qutb Shahi Hyderabad – indeed, it has become a virtual symbol of the city itself – the Charminar appears typologically unique, and does not fit readily into any established building category known from the medieval Indo-Muslim world.[2] Although its wide central arches and flanking minar towers call to mind the forms of a gateway, this "gateway" is not articulated with any wall, and it leads nowhere except into its own enigmatic interior, centred on a fountain (figure 2). Although it contains a small, exquisite mosque in its uppermost storey (figure 3), the building as a whole is clearly neither a mosque, nor simply just a grand platform for a mosque. In short, the functional identity of this monument is by no means readily apparent, and the building has been understood in many different ways in the centuries since its construction.[3]

The Charminar may be typologically unique, but its original significance may nonetheless be grasped if we consider the specific historical circumstances that surrounded its construction and examine the place of the monument within its larger urban context. Following these clues, it becomes apparent that the Charminar belongs to a well-defined Deccani architectural type – that of the *chaubara* or "four-fold

4

Charminar, outer arcade of the mezzanine level.

house" that marks the centre of the city – even though the specific form it takes marks a decisive departure from earlier documented examples of this building type. Consideration of the relationship between the Charminar and earlier forms of the *chaubara* sheds much light on the complex and productive interplay between Persianate architectural forms and ideas on the one hand, and those of the local, pre-Sultanate Deccani architectural tradition on the other.

Architectural Design

Before turning to the larger context of the Charminar, let us first pause to consider its architectural design (see figure 1). As experienced from outside at ground level, the Charminar is an essentially cubic structure that presents an alternating rhythm of interlocking voids and solids. Its four cardinal sides are relieved by spacious arches, great open spaces physically inviting movement inside, toward the centre of the building's domed chamber, while the

intervening corners present the contrast of the four minars that rise up over the core of the building and give it its name. These powerful solid forms not only pull the eye upward, but also afford actual access to the building's two upper storeys through spiral stairways contained within. Three rings of projecting arcaded balconies – the lowermost doubled – divide each minar into four levels, the uppermost crowned in each case by a dome sprouting from upturned lotus petals.

The first of the building's two upper storeys is essentially a mezzanine, with an arcade of seven arches providing views outward from each side, and a continuous circular line of sixteen arches inside, affording views down into the central space from a level just below the springing of the flattened dome (figures 4 and 5). The intervening space between these outer and inner arcades is divided into a succession of small, vaulted chambers of various shapes and sizes, but these are connected laterally so that it is possible

to move in continuous circumambulation around the central domed space at the core of the building. These chambers are arranged in two concentric series. The inner one is divided into four square chambers in the cardinal directions, and four octagonal ones at the corners; each of these chambers is connected, through lateral openings, across an intervening bay of irregular plan. The second ambulatory is divided up into 24 rectangular chambers (figure 6). Outside the outer arcade, there is a narrow projecting balcony with a low parapet, thus providing yet a third circuit around which the building can be circumambulated.

The uppermost storey is occupied by a small but sumptuously decorated mosque, tucked neatly into the square space between the minars. It consists of a covered prayer hall on the western side, and arcaded *riwaq*s or galleries on the other three sides. The facade of the prayer hall is articulated by an arcade of five bays, framed between projecting minarets at each corner (see figure 3). The arcade is doubled, with each

5

Charminar, interior mezzanine arcade.

6

Charminar, outer ambulatory of the mezzanine.

PHILLIP B. WAGONER

7

Charminar, stucco ornament
on two-storey entrance tower of
the mosque on upper storey.
Photograph: ACSAA Slide
#2388 © AAAUM.

pointed arch fronted by a second, multilobed arch richly decorated with carved stucco.[4] On the eastern side, on axis with the mihrab of the prayer hall, there is a domed, two-storeyed entrance tower, with equally fine carved stucco ornament (figure 7). The outer arcades of the mosque's *riwaq*s and prayer hall are fitted with delightfully varied stone grilles, but otherwise these arcades present themselves as a subtly modulated continuation of the outer arcades of the mezzanine level (see figure 4), thus making the mosque practically undetectable from the outside.

A Millennial *Chaubara*

Contemporary historical sources establish that the Charminar was constructed in the year AH 1000 (1591 CE), as the first building in Sultan Muhammad Quli Qutb Shah's new city of Hyderabad.[5] What is especially significant is that this date marks the beginning of the second Islamic millennium – an event that was widely celebrated in the Islamic world. The timing thus suggests that Hyderabad was deliberately founded as a "millennial" city, and this notion is further supported by the existence of an important album of Qutb Shahi calligraphy in the Chester Beatty Library in Dublin, known as "the Millennial Album". This work includes one page invoking blessings upon Sultan Muhammad Quli in the year AH 1000, and another recording a prayer marking the arrival of the new millennium.[6] Clearly, the year 1000 was viewed in the Deccan as a time of renewal, and was taken as

an especially appropriate time for new beginnings – such as the founding of a new capital city. Accordingly, the Sultan and his advisers selected a spot several kilometres to the east of Golconda, and began constructing the new capital on undeveloped land there. Significantly, the very first building erected in the new city was the Charminar. As the only building completed in the year of the city's foundation, it thus served to commemorate both the arrival of the millennium and the establishment of the new city.

Just as importantly, the Charminar also served to mark the centre of Hyderabad, providing a point of origin and reference point for the planning grid that determined its layout. Thus, a system of four axial roads proceeded outward toward the four quarters from this monumental crossing, in effect projecting the four-quartered geometry of the monument itself out into the surrounding urban fabric (figures 8 and 9). The building thus functioned as the central node in the city's armature, calling to mind the similarly designed *quadrifrons* of many imperial Roman cities.

The Charminar may embody a singular design, but it is by no means the first instance of a monument marking the centre of a sultanate city. Indeed, the Charminar appears to belong to a well-defined type of Deccani monument, the *chaubara* or "four-fold house", that is often found at the centre of medieval Deccani cities, marking the intersection of four cardinal avenues.[7] These *chaubara*s vary significantly in their design, even while they are identical with

8

The Golconda road, running
west from the Charminar.
Golconda Fort – the original
Qutb Shahi capital – can be
seen on the horizon, just to the
right of the end of the road.

9

The road to Koh-i Tur, running
south from Charminar.

respect to their situation and the idea of "quartering" referenced through their names. At Bidar, for example, which served as the capital of the Bahmani Sultanate from the mid-15th century, the lower town is structured by two main avenues, running roughly east–west and north–south, and the point of their intersection is occupied by a *chaubara* in the form of a tapering, circular tower (figure 10).[8] This tower rises some 21 metres above the ground – thus providing an excellent platform for surveillance – but it lacks any formal articulation accentuating the four-quartered conception revealed by its name. Another example of a Bahmani *chaubara* is preserved at Udgir, a major Bahmani stronghold in eastern Maharashtra, where the building similarly serves to anchor the crossing of the cardinal avenues in the lower town (figure 11). This *chaubara* is not as lofty as Bidar's – being only two storeys high – but it is octagonally planned and articulated by arches so as to express clearly its connection with the four quarters – and for that matter, with the four intermediate directions as well. There is also a *chaubara* at Kandhar – another Bahmani town in eastern Maharashtra – but here the original Bahmani structure has been completely replaced by modern construction.

Ultimately, the origins of the Deccani *chaubara* may be traced back to pre-sultanate architectural traditions in the region, and specifically to a variety of four-doored temple (variously termed *chaumukh* or *sarvatobhadra*) with cosmological, imperial associations. Perhaps the most important and influential example of this temple type was the shrine of Svayambhusiva, located at the centre of the city of Warangal, which served as the capital of the Kakatiya kingdom from the late 12th century until 1323.[9] This temple was not only four-doored – like the Charminar and, at least conceptually, like the various *chaubara*s – but more importantly, it was located at the centre of Warangal, close to the crossing of the cardinal avenues that structured this four-quartered city. Svayambhusiva was the patron divinity of the Kakatiya family, and was worshipped in the form of a four-faced linga enshrined at the centre of the temple, gazing out through its four doors and into the four quarters of the city over which he was lord (figure 12). Although the temple itself was demolished in 1323, when the Kakatiya kingdom was annexed by the Delhi Sultanate, the four monumental portals (*torana*) which had demarcated the boundaries of its ritual precinct were carefully preserved (figure 13).

10

The Bahmani *chaubara* at Bidar (Bidar district, Karnataka).

11

The Bahmani *chaubara* at Udgir (Latur district, Maharashtra).

These *torana*s continued to play an important role in the structuring of Sultanpur, as Warangal was renamed; they demarcated an open plaza at the centre of the city that was the location of an expansive Jami Masjid during the city's sultanate occupation. Warangal's four *torana*s thus provide an important link between pre-sultanate and sultanate expressions of the *chaubara* concept.[10]

Although pre-sultanate manifestations of the *chaubara* – like Warangal's Svayambhusiva Temple – had been clothed in the specific garb of traditional Hindu religious architecture, the *chaubara* remained in essence a non-sectarian expression of deeper Indic ideas of cosmic kingship. Ultimately, it was a planning device that served to proclaim the cosmic character of any city by marking its centre as the "pivot of the four quarters" – an embodiment of the axis mundi, the

Deccan. This point is driven home quite forcefully by the early Bijapuri illustrated manuscript *Nujum al-'Ulum*, a Persian treatise on astrology and kingship written and illustrated in 1570, just two decades before the construction of the Charminar. With its depictions of sultans on cosmic thrones, its multiple representations of *mandala*s and other cosmograms, and its detailed exposition of the treasures of the *cakravartin* or universal king, this manuscript provides eloquent testimony to the interest in traditional Indic notions of cosmic kingship at the sultanate courts of the Deccan.

12

Four-faced linga of Svayambhusiva, from the ruined Svayambhusiva Temple, Warangal (Warangal district, Andhra Pradesh).

The Interplay of Indic and Persianate Ideas

As a latter-day *chaubara*, the Charminar resonates deeply with traditional Indic cosmological ideas. At the same time, however, its specific form and conception reveal the impact of Islamic and Persianate ideas to a degree not seen in any earlier *chaubara*. In the first place, the Charminar is not oriented precisely to the cardinal directions, but exhibits a declination of 10 degrees, so that the four sides of the monument are oriented at 10, 100, 190, and 280 degrees. Clearly, this departure from perfect cardinality resulted from a concern that the mosque on the building's upper floor should be properly oriented toward the *qibla* of Mecca, which was interpreted as lying 10 degrees

point from which creation proceeded and order spread outward into the world. By occupying or controlling this place, a ruler ensured the ritual effectiveness of his kingship, and expressed his aspirations to become a *cakravartin* or universal emperor. If the ideas and rituals of cosmic kingship had been compelling to Hindu rulers in the pre-sultanate period, they certainly remained just as relevant and attractive to the Muslim sultans who succeeded them as overlords of the

13

One of the four *torana*s from the Svayambhusiva Temple at Warangal.

north of due west – that is, at 280 degrees – in some
other notable mosques in this part of the Deccan.[11]
The effect of this angular declination of the
monument is of course that the entire urban grid of
the city – which is projected from the central point of
the Charminar – comes to be oriented to the *qibla*.
For a city designed to commemorate the beginning

of the second Islamic millennium, a more suitable
orientation can hardly be imagined.

Strictly Islamic concerns, however, were not the
only ones to motivate the designers of this edifice.
Equally important was the pre-Islamic Iranian idea
of the *chahar-taq* – literally the "four arches" – which
served as a widespread symbolic image of the cosmos

in medieval Persian poetry. This literary symbol envisioned the universe as a domed quadrangular building of vast proportions, carried on four arches and illuminated at its apex by the sun as the light of heaven and earth; moreover, it often inspired formal expressions in diverse media, from small ceramic bowls and lamps to full-scale architectural monuments like throne rooms and tombs that literally replicated the *chahar-taq*'s four arches and celestial dome.[12] In casting Hyderabad's *chaubara* not as a circular or octagonal tower, but as an expansive four-arched structure vaulted inside by a dome with a solar lotus at its apex (figure 14), the designers of the Charminar appear to have seized upon the underlying similarities between Indic and Persianate conceptions of the cosmos. By creating a monument that was at once Indic, Persianate, and Islamic (figure 15), the Charminar's designers and patron have affirmed the fundamental commensurability of these diverse cultural traditions that flowed together so vitally in the Deccan's sultanate period.

NOTES

1.   For an excellent survey of Deccani Sultanate architecture, see George Michell and Mark Zebrowski, *Architecture and Art of the Deccan Sultanates* (Cambridge, 1999).

2.   There is in fact another building known as the Char Minar – this one in Bukhara in Uzbekistan. Like Hyderabad's Charminar, it is conceived as a domed square with four arches and four minarets marking the corners of the building. This building was not constructed until 1807, more than two centuries after the Charminar of Hyderabad. See Edgar Knobloch, *Monuments of Central Asia: A Guide to the Archaeology, Art, and Architecture of Turkestan* (London: I.B.Tauris, 2001), p. 128 and colour plate 67. A second structure in Bukhara that shares the Char Minar's conception is the small pavilion in the courtyard of the Mausoleum of Hazrat Baha al-din Naqshbandi (d. 1389). While the mausoleum itself dates from the 14th century, the age of this small pavilion is not known. See Knobloch, p. 130 and plate 40. Both of these buildings differ from the Charminar of Hyderabad in being single-storeyed, with the dome exposed on the exterior.

3.   It has been described variously as a madrasa or *khanqah*, a gateway to the Qutb Shahi palace, a water reservoir, a replica of a *taziyah* commemorating the end of an outbreak of cholera, and a replica of the shrine of Imam Ali al-Riza at Mashhad, intended as a surrogate for those who could not complete the physical pilgrimage. For an insightful and carefully documented review of these various interpretations, see H.K. Sherwani, *History of the Qutb Shahi Dynasty*, New Delhi: Munshiram Manoharlal, 1974, pp. 304–05.

4.   It should be noted that the carved stucco visible on the monument today is not the original 16th-century work, but dates from a renovation carried out under Asaf Jahi patronage in 1824 (AH 1258). See Syed Ali Asgar Bilgrami, *Landmarks of the Deccan:*

A Comprehensive Guide to the Archaeological Remains of the City and Suburbs of Hyderabad (Hyderabad: Government Press, 1927), p. 19. In general stylistic character, however, it relates closely to actual Qutb Shahi work; it appears likely that the original decorative scheme and motifs were followed closely in the 19th-century renovation.

5.   Bilgrami, *Landmarks of the Deccan*, p. 17; Sherwani, *History of the Qutb Shahi Dynasty*, p. 302.

6.   David James, "The Millennial Album of Muhammad-Quli Qutb Shah", *Islamic Art: An Annual Dedicated to the Art and Culture of the Islamic World* II (1987), pp. 243–54.

7.   The conceptual similarity between the Charminar and Bidar's Chaubara was first noted by Sherwani, *History of the Qutb Shahi Dynasty*, p. 305.

8.   Although local tradition avers that this *chaubara* dates to Bidar's pre-Islamic period, in its present form it most likely dates primarily to the time of Bidar's rebuilding as the Bahmani capital, at the beginning of the reign of Sultan Ahmad Shah-i al-Wali (r. 1422–36). See Ghulam Yazdani, *Bidar: Its History and Monuments* (London: Oxford University Press, 1947), pp. 90–91.

9.   For reconstruction and discussion of the Warangal temple, see Phillip B. Wagoner and John Henry Rice, "From Delhi to the Deccan: Newly Discovered Tughluq Monuments at Warangal-Sultanpur and the Beginnings of Indo-Islamic Architecture in Southern India," *Artibus Asiae* LXI/1(2001), pp. 77–117 (see especially pp. 109–11).

10.   Wagoner and Rice, "From Delhi to the Deccan"; Phillip B. Wagoner, "The Place of Warangal's *Kirti-Toranas* in the History of Indian Islamic Architecture", *Religion and the Arts* 8/1(2004), pp. 6–36.

11.   The ruined Tughluq Jami Masjid of Warangal-Sultanpur was likewise oriented to a *qibla* of 280 degrees. As David King has pointed out, local understandings of *qibla*-orientation often changed significantly from one period to the next. See David A. King, *World-Maps for Finding the Direction and Distance to Mecca: Innovation and Tradition in Islamic Science* (Leiden: Brill, 1999), pp. 124–27. Indeed, in Hyderabad itself, the Jami Masjid built by Sultan Muhammad Quli a few years later did not conform to the *qibla* grid established by his Charminar, but was oriented to a *qibla* of approximately 270 degrees. See S.P. Shorey, "Hyderabad: Garden to a City", in *Golconda and Hyderabad,* ed. Shehbaz H. Safrani (Bombay: Marg, 1992), p. 20.

12.   Assadullah Souren Melikian-Chirvani, "The Light of Heaven and Earth: From the *Chahar-taq* to the *Mihrab*", *Bulletin of the Asia Institute* (Detroit), new series, 4(1990): 95–131.

PHOTO CREDITS

All photographs by the author, unless otherwise mentioned.

Index

Page numbers in **bold** refer to captions